C++: An Introduction for Experienced C Programmers

C++: An Introduction for Experienced C Programmers

Rex Jaeschke

CBM
BOOKS

Copyright © 1993 Rex Jaeschke

All rights reserved. No part of this publication may be reproduced, stored in a retrieval system, or transmitted in any form or by any means whatsoever, except in the case of brief quotations embodied in critical reviews and articles.

The information in this book is subject to change without notice and should not be construed as a commitment by the author or the publisher. Although every precaution has been taken in the preparation of this book, the author and publisher assume no responsibility for errors or omissions.

Printed in the United States of America.

Cover design by Michael Cousart.

Library of Congress Cataloging-in-Publication Data

Jaeschke, Rex.
    C++ : an introduction for experienced C programmers / Rex Jaeschke.
       p.   cm.
    Includes index.
    ISBN 1-878956-27-2
    1. C++ (Computer program language)   I. Title.
QA76.73.C15J3354 1993
005.13'3–dc20   92-30284
                                                            CIP

Please address comments and questions to the publisher:

CBM Books
A Division of Cardinal Business Media, Inc.
101 Witmer Road
Horsham, PA 19044
(215) 957-1500
FAX (215) 957-1050
CompuServe: 76702,1565
Internet: 76702.1565@compuserve.com

This book was typeset by the author using the TeX typesetting package, LaTeX macros, and Makeindex indexing tool. Final copy was printed at 2,000 dpi using Computer Modern fonts.

Contents

Preface	ix

I C++ As A Better C 1

1 The Basics 3
Comments 3
Identifiers 3
Basic I/O 3
Function Definitions and Prototypes 5
Predefined Macros 6
Type-Safe Linkage 6
Declarations 8
Cast Operator 9
Scope Resolution Operator 10
`const` Type Qualifier 11
Anonymous Unions 11
Enumerated Types 12

2 Functions 15
Overloading Functions 15
Default Argument Values 20
Inline Functions 22

3 Dynamic Memory Allocation 27
Introduction to Memory Allocation 27
Handling `new` Errors 30

4 References 33
Introduction to References 33
Passing Arguments by Reference 34
Functions that Return References 38
References Outside Function Calls 39
References Versus Pointers 45

II Using Existing Class Libraries   47

5 Standard Class Libraries   49
Introduction to Classes 49
String Manipulation 50
Complex Numbers 56

6 Input and Output   59
Format Control 59
Stream Member Functions 64
File I/O 67
String Encoding and Decoding 70
User-Defined Manipulators 72

III Writing Your Own Simple Classes   75

7 Classes and Objects   77
Introduction to Classes 77
Data Privacy 78
Member Functions 79
Restricted Global Data 84
`static` Member Functions 86
`const`- and `volatile`-Qualified Member Functions 87
Enumerated Types and `typedefs` 90
Classes, Structures, and Unions 91
Nested Classes 92
Relaxing Class Member Access Restrictions 95
Pointers to Class Members 96
Exercise 1 102

8 Member Functions Revisited   103
Passing Objects to Member Functions 103
Overloading Member Functions 106
Exercise 2 109
Default Argument Values 110
Exercise 3 112
Inline Member Functions 112
Exercise 4 118

9 Constructors and Destructors   119
Constructors 119
Destructors 121
Aggregates Containing Objects 123
Initializing Reference and `const` Members 124

| Constructors in Nested Classes 126
     Static Data and Execution Order 129
     The Effects of Changing Control Flow 133
     Temporary Objects 134
     Dynamically Allocated Objects 135
     Exercise 5 140
     Exercise 6 141
     Exercise 7 141

10 Operator Overloading   **143**
     Introduction to Operator Overloading 143
     Some Simple Examples 145
     Exercise 8 147
     List Class 147
     Overloading Unary Operators 152
     Exercise 9 155
     Overloading [ ] 155
     Overloading ( ) 157
     Class-Specific Versions of `new` and `delete` 159
     Overloading the I/O Operators << and >> 161
     Exercise 10 165
     Assigning and Copying Class Objects 165
     Conversion Functions 170
     Rules of Thumb 171
     Exercise 11 172

IV   Beyond Simple Classes   173

11 Advanced Topics   **175**
     Templates 175
     Inheritance 175
     Exception Handling 176

V   Appendixes   177

A Operator Precedence   **179**

B Keywords   **181**

C Compatibility With Old Releases   **183**

D C and C++ Compatibility Issues   **185**

E	Solutions to Exercises	187
	Exercise 1	187
	Exercise 2	192
	Exercise 3	197
	Exercise 4	200
	Exercise 5	207
	Exercise 6	210
	Exercise 7	212
	Exercise 8	214
	Exercise 9	216
	Exercise 10	223

Recommended Reading   **227**

Index   **229**

Preface

This book is intended to allow experienced C programmers to get started with C++ relatively quickly. The easy, conversational style makes it suitable for use as a self-paced training book. In fact, I wrote it with teaching in mind. The narrative and the problems with their worked-out solutions were designed to be suitable for use as a 5-day seminar covering 30 hours, including labs.

C++ programmers can be divided into two main groups: those who will simply use C++ as a "better C" or primarily will use class libraries written by others, and those who will develop and maintain class libraries. I like to think of the first group as consumers or users of classes and the second as producers of classes. This book addresses primarily the first of these two groups. I recognize, however, that inevitably, some users of classes will want to implement classes of their own. Specifically, this book does not provide detailed coverage of the following topics: inheritance, polymorphism, and templates. Exception handling also has been omitted because of its advanced nature and the fact that its definition is still evolving. While these are important topics, a discussion of them is inappropriate in an introductory text such as this. By eliminating coverage of these topics, I can devote more space to helping the C programmer make the transition to C++, while keeping the size of the book manageable.

The chapters of the book are organized as follows:

Part I. C++ As A Better C

> Chapters 1 through 4 identify the additions and improvements, which do not involve object-oriented programming, that C++ makes to C.

Part II. Using Existing Class Libraries

> Chapters 5 and 6 introduce you to the bare minimum amount of information you need to know about classes in order to use well-documented existing class libraries, including the Standard C++ I/O library.

Part III. Writing Your Own Simple Classes

> Chapters 7 through 1 present the evolutionary design of a simple class called `Circle`, as well as parts of a string and vector class. To reinforce the material, lab exercises are presented at the end of some sections. These exercises involve the design and use of a simple date class. Solutions are contained in appendix E.

Part IV. Beyond Simple Classes

> Chapter 11 gives a brief summary of templates, inheritance, and exception handling.

Part V. Appendixes

> Appendixes A through E present the operator precedence table, a table of keywords, a technical summary of important changes made in various releases of C++ from AT&T, important ways in which C++ is not a proper superset of Standard C, and worked solutions to the lab exercises.

This book is not directly about class design but rather about using classes and being able to understand the documented interface to the classes for which you have access. The standard I/O classes described in `<iostream.h>` and related headers, and possibly classes defined in other headers you will use, make use of inheritance. Some may also use templates. However, if the user documentation for these classes is adequate, you should be able to use them without knowing much, if anything, about inheritance or templates.

Most books on C++ that I have seen try to cover the whole language and all levels of readers. I intentionally set out to limit the scope of this book for the following reasons:

- You can write a very large amount of useful code without using or even knowing all of C++. In many cases, C++ is being used (at least initially) simply as a "better C."

- You have to learn to crawl before you can walk. All C++ programmers must learn how to use classes before they will have much success at designing them.

- Currently, most C++ programmers are coming from a C environment. The fact that C++ is so popular and that it builds on the syntax of C makes many C programmers view C++ somehow as the logical successor to C. Thus, I expect the reader to be well-versed in C, particularly in the areas of prototypes, structures, and type qualifiers, as well as in the strengths and weaknesses of that language.

- It has been my experience that most programmers coming to C++ have no formal training in object-oriented programming and likely will not receive any. In fact, they might not even care much about object-oriented programming at all.

- Most C++ programmers will likely get by very nicely without having to design many (if any) classes themselves. They will view class libraries much in the same way they do object libraries—as a black box that somehow magically does what is needed.

- Designing a nontrivial class, and doing it correctly, can be a complex, time-consuming, and iterative process. It requires a good deal of experience, technical expertise, and mastery of the art of abstraction.

- For users to derive from an existing class, they must have many of the same skills needed to design the class in the first place.

You might disagree with some (or even many) items in this list of statements. However, there is no one correct set of reasons for using a particular programming language. Indeed, C and C++ are being used for many applications and by many programmers for which they are not particularly well-suited.

Frankly, I have found much of the literature on object-oriented programming in general, and C++ in particular, to be esoteric and somewhat intimidating. As a result, I have tried to cut through the hype, using terms that everyday C programmers can understand and relate to.

Finally, I am not yet convinced that anything new has really been invented in object-oriented programming these last 20 years. What is new is that many old and good ideas are now being supported within, and enforced directly by, languages. For whatever reason, object-oriented programming is currently fashionable again, this time in the guise of C++. And having an object-oriented programming language ride on the coattails of an extremely popular language such as C helps propel C++ even further. From my humble perspective, for the large part, C++ provides a better C, particularly in the way it can help manage large projects. And it encourages programmers to get the discipline they should have had to program in C in the first place but did not have. As for those coming from the non-C world, I suggest they buy into a language built on top of a much safer one, such as Pascal. I see no point in dragging non-C programmers through all the trials and tribulations of C just to get to C++'s object-oriented programming. There are already far too many programmers being overwhelmed by C without adding more, and there *are* other commercially viable languages that support object-oriented programming.

A Release History of C++

Since the original version of C++, known as Release 1.0 or more simply as R1.0, AT&T (and now UNIX System Laboratories Inc.) has issued numerous revisions. R2.0 saw the addition of a whole new replacement for the I/O library. R2.1 tightened up the language definition and even made some changes that were incompatible with previous releases. R3.0 added support for templates. The formal description of R2.1 was used as one of the base documents by the committee currently drafting the C++ standard. (The other base document was the C standard.) A full description of R2.1 is available in *The Annotated C++ Reference Manual* from Addison-Wesley, by Margaret A. Ellis and Bjarne Stroustrup. This text is commonly referred to as "The ARM."

There are a number of incompatibilities between R2.1 (and R3.0) and earlier releases. They are documented in appendix C.

As of this writing, most commercially available compilers are aimed at R2.1, so that is the release on which this book is based. As the primary addition to R3.0 was support for templates, and this topic is outside the scope of this book, R2.1 conformance will suffice.

The Future of C++

It is clear from the user and vendor momentum that C++ is here to stay as a tool for programming in general and object-oriented programming in particular. With the advent of a standard, for the most part, the discrepancies that exist between implementations hopefully will disappear, and any missing pieces will be provided.

As to whether C++ will be viewed as the logical successor to C, only time will tell. While this will be true for some people, it will not necessarily be true for all or even the majority of C programmers. In any event, the C and C++ standards are being developed by different committees. And while C++ is in the process of being standardized, Standard C is in the process of being extended on various fronts.

Acknowledgments

Many thanks go to the reviewers of this book: Nelson Beebe, Bryan Higgs, Mike Holly, Aron Insinga, Bob Jervis, Gene Oleynik, and John Wittig. Richard A. Wells also provided valuable technical input and was instrumental in causing a major reorganization of chapters and sections.

To the staff at CBM Books, many thanks. In particular, thanks to Annette Nelson, Patty Wall, and Roseann Brooks.

Numerous vendors provided review copies of their compilers and access to their support staff. These included the following: Borland International Inc. (Borland C++), Digital Equipment Corp. (DEC C++), JPI TopSpeed Consortium Inc. (TopSpeed C++), Metaware Inc. (High C/C++), Microsoft Corp. (Microsoft C++), and Symantec Corp. (Zortech C++). Each time I took delivery of a new compiler, I used it to compile all of the examples from the book. And each time, I found subtle and not-so-subtle bugs in my examples, in the new compiler, and even in all the other compilers. With some examples, there was considerable disagreement among the compilers as to whether the example actually contained errors. In those few cases where the draft standard itself was unclear, I decided to drop the example.

This book was reviewed in manuscript form by students attending my "Introduction to C++" seminars. They made many helpful suggestions and asked a lot of questions that resulted in changes or additions in the text and examples. Having taught seminars based on this text for more than a year, I am happy to report that it appears to be appropriate for the audience to which it is aimed.

Part I
C++ As A Better C

Chapter 1

The Basics

C++ contains a number of relatively minor, but useful, enhancements to C. These enhancements are introduced in this chapter.

Comments

C++ supports an alternate form of comment. For example:

```
// This program counts records

int count = 0;          // Total count of transactions
```

Each comment starts with //. This form of comment is line-oriented and ends at the end of the source line on which it begins. C++ continues to support C-style comments. //-style comments can be nested inside /* ... */.

Identifiers

Unlike C, in C++ *all* characters in an identifier are significant. However, the C++ standards committee is considering setting an actual (but nontrivial) minimum limit.

Identifiers containing two consecutive underscores are reserved for use by implementations.

Basic I/O

C++ has its own machinery for performing I/O. It involves using the header iostream.h[1]. All I/O is done to or from a *stream*, and that stream is connected to a device or file. Here is an example:

---
[1] Some C++ implementations require C++-specific headers to have names with a suffix of .hxx or .hpp instead of .h. The form .h will be used throughout this book.

```
#include <iostream.h>

main()
{
        int i;
        double d;
        char c;

        cout << "Enter i, d, and c: ";
        cin >> i >> d >> c;
        cout << "\ni = " << i << ", d = " << d;
        cout << ", c = " << c << '\n';

        return 0;
}
```

Some sample input and the corresponding output are:

```
Enter i, d, and c: 100 1.23 A
i = 100, d = 1.23, c = A
```

Just as C provides the predefined `FILE` pointers `stdin`, `stdout`, and `stderr`, C++ provides equivalent predefined streams `cin`, `cout`, and `cerr`. To direct output to a stream, we use the `<<` operator. This is called *insertion*. Ordinarily, this operator means bit-shift left. However, C++ permits most operators to be *overloaded*. That is, they can be given different meanings in different contexts. In the example above, the inclusion of the header `iostream.h` caused the `<<` operator to be overloaded and made suitable for use in I/O. (The details of I/O operator overloading are discussed in chapter 1, "Operator Overloading.") Similarly, we can read from `cin` using the `>>` operator. This is known as *extraction*.

As shown above, we can output multiple values in the same statement. In the case of `'\n'`, we could have used `"\n"` instead, as `cout` knows how to handle all the built-in scalar types as well null-terminated arrays of `char`. Unlike `printf`, `cout` does not need to be told which conversion specifier to use. By using the information it finds in `iostream.h`, along with the types of the objects being output, the compiler can choose the appropriate display format. You can, however, override the default format. Note that expressions of type `char`, `signed char`, or `unsigned char` are output as characters, not integers. Also, the floating-point value is displayed with only the number of significant digits needed.

Unlike `scanf`, `cin` does not need the addresses of the input variables to be given. Since the compiler can detect when an input value is to be stored into a scalar, it can arrange for the address to be used. In fact, we must not use the `&` operator in this context.

Like most of `scanf`'s conversion specifiers, the `>>` operator skips leading white space. And when reading in strings, it stops on embedded white space.

`cerr` is much like `cout`. However, the latter is buffered while the former is not. A buffered version of standard error, called `clog`, is also provided. The difference between the two is quite important; if a program terminates abnormally, buffered output streams might not be flushed.

C++ permits most of its operators to be overloaded. However, a given operator always has the same precedence and associativity, as defined in the language. That is, even though << has been overloaded in the following example, the << operator still associates right to left:

```
#include <iostream.h>

main()
{
/*1*/     cout << 1 << 5 << "\n";
/*2*/     cout << (1 << 5) << "\n";
/*3*/     cout << (5 ? 10 : 20) << "\n";

          return 0;
}
```

The output produced is:

```
15
32
10
```

In case 1, << was intended to be used for two different purposes: as both a left-shift and an output operator. To get the correct answer, however, you need grouping parentheses, as shown in case 2. You also need them in case 3, since without them << has higher precedence than ?:, and a compilation error results. In I/O statements, then, the rule is to use grouping parentheses around expressions containing operators with precedence equal to or less than that of << and >>.

I/O is discussed in detail in chapter 6, "Input and Output."

Function Definitions and Prototypes

Non-void Functions

In both C and C++, the return type of main is int. However, in C we often do not return a value, which generally results in undefined, but acceptable, behavior. With C++, a non-void function, such as main, must return a value. (Some C++ compilers might issue a warning rather than an error for this so that they can be backward-compatible with Standard C.)

Old-Style Declarations

In C++, the function declarations void f() and void f(void) are equivalent. In C, they are not, since the first declares a function taking an unknown number of arguments while the second declares a function taking no arguments.

Default Function Typing

In C, if the expression that precedes the parenthesized argument list in a function call consists solely of an identifier, and if no declaration is visible for this identifier, the identifier is implicitly declared exactly as if the declaration **extern int** *identifier* (); appeared in the innermost block containing the function call. That is, the function is assumed to return an **int** and no argument list checking is performed.

C++ does not make this assumption. Instead, it requires either a declaration or definition of that function before the first reference to its name.

Predefined Macros

The macro __cplusplus is guaranteed to be predefined for all C++ compilers, which allows C++-specific code to be conditionally compiled.

Type-Safe Linkage

The addition of function prototypes to C++ (and then to Standard C) was a step in the right direction because it checked that functions were called consistently. However, the use of prototypes does not completely guarantee that functions are called correctly. Consider the following example:

```
// source file 1

#include <iostream.h>

int f(double d);

main()
{
        cout << f(1.2) << '\n';

        return 0;
}
// source file 2

#include <iostream.h>

void f(int i, unsigned long ul)
{
        cout << i * ul << '\n';
}
```

In source file 1, the call to function f matches the prototype. However, neither matches the definition of f in source file 2. In C, this mismatch would go undetected. However, in C++, this produces a linker error to the effect that no function was found that matched the call in source file 1.

When these files are compiled, the external names generated for the call to f and those generated for the definition of f are different. For example, one compiler assigned the name _f_Nd for the function f declared in source file 1, and the name _f_NiUl for the one defined in source file 2. Each external name was constructed from the function name, followed by letters that indicate the number and type of arguments. The process by which identifiers are converted to unique external names is called *name mangling*. The scheme used can vary from one implementation to another[2], in which case it can be impossible to link object modules created by different compilers running on the same system. In the case of arguments having structure, union, or enumerated types, or pointers thereto, the corresponding tag name is usually encoded in the mangled name as well.

We refer to the unique combination of a function's name and its argument list as that function's *signature*. A function's signature does not include its return type, however.

In the example above, the two names f are mangled differently, resulting in the linker seeing a call to a function for which there was no corresponding definition. The linker would also see a function definition for which there was no reference. This mangling and checking of names is known as *type-safe linkage*.

Name mangling can be disabled. One reason to do this is to call functions written in languages other than C++. For example, C++ implementations include the Standard C headers (such as **string.h**) and their corresponding object libraries. To call **strcpy**, for example, you still include the parent header. However, inside the header, mangling typically is disabled as follows:

```
#ifdef __cplusplus
extern "C" {
        char *strcpy(char *__dest, const char *__src);
}
#endif
```

C++-supplied headers that declare C functions will use conditional-compilation directives to include or exclude the **extern** keyword, the string, and the braces. By testing whether __cplusplus is defined, we can tell if the header is being compiled by a C or C++ compiler.

The keyword **extern** is followed by a string that indicates the linkage to be used for the given function. The meaning of strings other than "C" and "C++" is implementation-defined, but support for these two strings, at least, is required. If the braces are used, they delimit a set of one or more external declarations. Without the braces, the linkage applies only to the next external declaration. This approach applies to both external data and functions. Such a linkage specification has file scope.

You cannot specify function linkage when you define a pointer to a function. Therefore, calling a function with non-C++ linkage via a pointer produces undefined behavior, although it will almost certainly work for "C" linkage.

---

[2]The ARM, §7.2.1c "Function Name Encoding," presents a scheme for encoding function names.

Declarations

Position

C requires that, inside a block, declarations must precede executable statements. C++ permits declarations to be located among executable statements as long as identifiers are declared before their first use. For example:

```
int test(int i)
{
        if (i < 0)
                return 0;

        int j = 5;

        return j * i;
}
```

Inside for Loops

Often, you need a variable simply to control the iteration of a loop. To accommodate this, C++ has extended the `for` loop to allow a local variable to be declared. For example:

```
void f()
{
        for (int index = 0; index < 10; ++index)
                // ...
}
```

The variable `index` is defined within the first "expression" of the `for` construct. The scope of this name extends to the end of the block enclosing the `for` statement, not just to the end of the loop body.

Use of Tag Names

C requires that once a structure, union, or enumerated type has been defined with a tag, that tag always must be preceded by the keyword `struct`, `union`, or `enum` even, though tags have a name space separate from other identifiers. C++ allows these keywords to be omitted in subsequent references to these types. For example:

```
struct Complex {
        double real;
        double imag;
};

Complex c;               // 'struct' keyword not needed
```

```
enum Color {red, blue, green};

Color house, car;        // 'enum' keyword not needed
```

This avoids the need to use **typedef** to achieve the same result.

Scope of Tag Names

In C and C++, structure and union definitions may be nested. For example:

```
struct s {
        union u {
                int i;
                double d;
        } u1;
        int j;
};

struct s s2;     // OK
union u u2;      // tag u not in scope
```

However, while this example will compile with C, it is not valid in C++. In C++, the tag u is specific to its parent structure type and is not visible outside that context. The same restriction applies to enumerated types, and their enumeration constants, defined inside a structure or union.

These nested type names can be accessed by using the scope resolution operator, which is discussed later in this chapter.

Cast Operator

C++ supports the C-style of casting, using the form:

    (*type*) *expression*

It also supports a style that uses *functional notation*, which has the form:

    type (*expression*)

The functional notation approach has a minor limitation, however: *type* must be a simple type (that is, one consisting of a single keyword only) or a typedef name. For example:

```
#include <iostream.h>

typedef unsigned int Uint;
typedef void *VP;
```

```
main()
{
        cout << unsigned int(1.2) << '\n';      // error
        cout << unsigned(1.2) << '\n';          // OK, single keyword
        cout << Uint(1.2) << '\n';              // OK, typedef name

        cout << void *("ABC") << '\n';          // error
        cout << VP("ABC") << '\n';              // OK, typedef name

        return 0;
}
```

Scope Resolution Operator

Both C and C++ permit the same identifier to be used in nested scopes. However, in C, only the inner-level declaration is available within that inner block. C++ provides access to the outermost-level declaration as well, as follows:

```
#include <iostream.h>

int i = 10;                             // block level 0

main()
{
        int i = 20;                     // block level 1

        // ...

                {
                        int i = 30;     // block level 2

                        cout << i << ", " << ::i << '\n';
                }

        return 0;
}
```

The output produced is:

```
30, 10
```

The scope resolution operator :: is used to access the variable i at block level 0. The variable i defined at block level 1 is not accessible from block level 2.

This operator is also used to qualify access to nested structures, unions, and enumerated type definitions. For example:

```
    struct s {
        enum color {red, blue, green} e;
        union u {
            int i;
            double d;
        } u1;
    };

    s::u u2;
    s::color paint = s::blue;
```

The tags color and u, and the enumeration constants red, blue, and green, are not visible outside the structure type s. However, they still can be accessed as long as the scope resolution operator is used, as shown in the definitions of u2 and paint.

If a structure, union, or enumerated type is nested more than one level deep, multiple scope resolution operators are needed. For example, s1::s2::s3 refers to the type s3, which is nested inside the type s2, which in turn, is nested inside type s1.

const Type Qualifier

In C++, when const is used in a file-scope object definition, it has semantics beyond those provided by C. Consider the following example:

```
    const int size = 6;

    int c[size];
```

In this example, size is used in a context in which a compile-time integer constant expression is needed, and size has this property[3].

If the const declaration does not contain extern, the object has internal linkage and there must be an initializer.

Even if the address of the object is taken, the object can be treated as a constant, just like a simple object-like macro.

Anonymous Unions

C++ supports the notion of an *anonymous union*. Such a union has no tag name, and its definition does not also define objects of that union type. Consider the following example:

```
    /*1*/   static union {int i; double d;};        // anonymous union
    /*2*/   union {int i; double d;} u1;
    /*3*/   typedef union {int i; double d;} un;
```

---

[3]The formal definition of C++ only guarantees this for integer objects, however.

```
void f()
{
/*4*/   i = 1;              // use anonymous int
/*5*/   d = 1.2;            // use anonymous double

/*6*/   u1.i = 1;
/*7*/   u1.d = 1.2;

/*8*/   un u0;
/*9*/   u0.i = 1;
/*10*/  u0.d = 1.2;
}
```

In case 1, a union having no tag is defined. Also, no identifiers are declared to have that type. In C, such a definition would be useless, since it could not be used anywhere. However, in C++, this is called an anonymous union, and it results in an unnamed object of unknown union type being created. Anonymous unions defined at file scope must explicitly be declared **static**. Members of anonymous unions are accessed directly by name, as shown in cases 4 and 5, and therefore, their names must be distinct from other identifiers in the same scope.

In case 2, a union type having no tag is defined. However, an identifier is declared to have that unknown union type. This is not an anonymous union, but rather it is a named object of an unknown union type. Cases 3 and 8 together produce the same effect as case 2. That is, using a type synonym for a tagless union type can also result in a named object of an unknown union type.

As an anonymous union has no name, it cannot be manipulated as a whole, and expressions of its unknown type cannot be formed.

Enumerated Types

C treats enumerated types as integral types, thereby allowing numerous illogical combinations of the two. C++ requires that such illogical uses be diagnosed, as it treats enumerated types as being distinct from integral types yet permits conversion between the two in the useful cases. The following example demonstrates some of this checking:

```
#include <iostream.h>

enum color1 {black, white} c1 = black;
enum color2 {red, green, blue} c2 = green;

void f(color1 e);

main()
{
/*1*/   c1 = 0;             // error, even though black == 0
/*2*/   c1 = white;
```

```
/*3*/   c1 = blue;      // error, incompatible types
/*4*/   c2 = white;     // error, incompatible types
/*5*/   c2 = blue;
/*6*/   c1 = c2;        // error, incompatible types


/*7*/   f(c1);
/*8*/   f(black);
/*9*/   f(0);           // error, incompatible types
/*10*/  f(red);         // error, incompatible types

        return 0;
}
```

Under certain circumstances, enumerated types are not compatible with integer types. In particular, an object of enumerated type may take on only a value of its own type or of an enumeration constant of that type. As such, c1 may not be initialized with the **int** zero, the enumeration constant **blue**, or c2. Note that in C, enumeration constants share the same name space as ordinary identifiers and are not restricted as they are in C++.

Similarly, type compatibility is checked across function calls, since these are defined in terms of assignment.

Note the explicit cast in case 11:

```
void f(color1 e)
{
/*11*/  cout << (int)e << '\n';
}
```

In C++, enumerated type objects are not synonyms for integer types, but they can be converted to integer types. The compiler can implicitly convert an enumerated type to the signed and unsigned versions of **int** and **unsigned int**. And while **iostream.h** defines the << operator for these types, the compiler does not know which one to pick. Therefore, without the cast, the usage is ambiguous. (The operator << can be overloaded to handle enumerated types directly, as we shall see in chapter 1, "Operator Overloading.")

Chapter 2

Functions

C++ contains a number of significant improvements to C, with regard to functions. These enhancements are function overloading, default argument values, and inlining. Each of these will be introduced in this chapter.

Overloading Functions

Introduction to Function Overloading

Overloading is a term used quite often in discussions about programming languages. Essentially, when something is overloaded, it takes on a number of possible meanings, depending on the context in which it occurs. For example, in the expression a + b, if a and b have type int, the plus is interpreted as "add two ints." However, if a and b have type double, the plus means "add two doubles." That is, the plus operator is overloaded.

Some languages also overload functions. For example, in FORTRAN, the square root function has the same name regardless of the arithmetic type of its argument. C, on the other hand, requires a unique version of each function type. For example, sqrt expects and returns a double; sqrtf expects and returns a float; and sqrtl expects and returns a long double.

There are two distinct schools of thought regarding function overloading: One says that each function should have its own unique name; the other says that there should be one generic function name shared by all functions having the same purpose, and the compiler should work out what to do itself. C follows the first approach and places the burden on the programmer, while C++ follows the second and places the burden on the implementation or, more correctly, on the designer of the functions.

There are two reasonable restrictions on function overloading in C++. The function main cannot be overloaded, nor can functions be declared as having non-C++ linkage.

The following program contains three versions of a function called myabs. That is, myabs is overloaded:

```
#include <iostream.h>

double myabs(double arg);
long myabs(long arg);
int myabs(int arg);

main()
{
        double d = myabs(1.2);
        long l = myabs(-50000L);
        int i = myabs(-5);

        cout << "d = " << d << ", l = " << l << ", i = " << i << '\n';

        return 0;
}

double myabs(double arg)
{
        return (arg < 0 ? -arg : arg);
}

long myabs(long arg)
{
        return (arg < 0 ? -arg : arg);
}

int myabs(int arg)
{
        return (arg < 0 ? -arg : arg);
}
```

The output produced is:

```
d = 1.2, l = 50000, i = 5
```

The compiler takes care of generating unique external names for each version of `myabs`. Consider the following example:

```
#include <iostream.h>

void f(int i);
void f(char c);
```

```
main()
{
/*1*/   f('A');
/*2*/   f(int('A'));

        return 0;
}

void f(char c)
{
        cout << "char version\n";
}

void f(int i)
{
        cout << "int version\n";
}
```

The output produced is:

```
char version
int version
```

In case 1, the character constant argument results in the `char` version of `f` being called. The reason for this is that in C++, the type of a character constant is `char`, whereas in C, it has type `int`. To call the `int` version of `f` using a character constant as the argument, you need an explicit cast, as used in case 2.

Argument Matching Rules

If each version of an overloaded function has a different number of arguments, selecting one of them for any given function call is easy. However, it can be much more complicated when multiple versions of a function have signatures that differ only in type. In such cases, the compiler must match each argument being passed with the corresponding argument in each prototype. This process is known as *argument matching*. The best-matching function is the intersection of all functions that best match on each argument. This intersection must result in one function only; otherwise, the call is invalid. The argument-matching steps are:

1. Exact match. This includes allowing type qualifiers in the prototype without having them on the actual arguments being passed.

2. Match after applying the usual integral and `float-to-double` promotions.

3. Match after standard conversion.

4. Match with ellipses.

Consider the following example:

```
#include <iostream.h>

void f1(int i, float f)    { cout << "f1a\n"; }
void f1(char C, double d)  { cout << "f1b\n"; }

void f2(int i, float f)    { cout << "f2a\n"; }
void f2(int i, int *pi)    { cout << "f2b\n"; }
void f2(int i, ...)        { cout << "f2c\n"; }

main()
{
/*1*/    f1(10, 1.2F);          // OK
/*2*/    f1(10, 1.2);           // error
/*3*/    f1('a', 1.2F);         // error
/*4*/    f1('a', 'b');          // OK
/*5*/    f2(1.2, "abc");        // OK

         return 0;
}
```

In case 1, there is an exact match for each argument, resulting in function `f1a` being called. Cases 2 and 3 match more than one prototype equally as well; both match one argument but require the other to be promoted or demoted. The call is therefore ambiguous. Case 4 matches the function `f1b`, and case 5 matches `f2c`.

The argument-matching rules are nontrivial. As a result, there can be some uncertainty in the programmer's mind as to which function will be selected in a given case. Therefore, you must be disciplined if you wish to keep overloaded functions manageable.

Pointers to Overloaded Functions

When an overloaded function is called, the argument list is used to determine which of the overloaded set is to be invoked. However, when the address of a function is taken, no argument list is present. It is possible, though, to take the address of an overloaded function, as long as there is sufficient context information available. This is always the case in initializations, assignments, function argument lists, and `return` statements. For example:

```
#include <iostream.h>

void f();
void f(double d);
```

```
        void (*g(void (*arg)()))();      // Function g takes a function ptr
                                          // as an argument and returns a function
                                          // pointer of the same type, by value.

        main()
        {
/*1*/       void (*pfv)() = &f;
/*2*/       void (*pfd)(double) = &f;

/*3*/       pfv = &f;
            (*pfv)();

/*4*/       pfd = &f;
            (*pfd)(123.456);

/*5*/       (*g(f))();

            return 0;
        }
```

In cases 1 through 4, the type of the pointer being initialized or assigned to includes a function signature. This signature is used to determine the appropriate version of f that is to be used. Case 5 calls the function whose address is returned from function g. The address passed to g is determined by the signature given in the prototype for that function.

The rest of the program follows:

```
        void f()
        {
                cout << "Inside f(void)\n";
        }

        void f(double d)
        {
                cout << "Inside f(double)\n";
        }

        void (*g(void (*arg)()))()
        {
/*6*/       return f;
        }
```

In case 6, the address returned is determined by the signature given in the declaration for that function.

Default Argument Values

Introduction to Default Arguments

C++ allows a function to be called with any leading part of the expected argument list, provided default values are defined for the unspecified trailing arguments. For example:

```
#include <iostream.h>

void test(int i = 4, long l = 6);

main()
{
/*1*/    test(5, 4);
/*2*/    test(5);
/*3*/    test();

         return 0;
}
void test(int i, long l)
{
         cout << "i = " << i << ", l = " << l << '\n';
}
```

The output produced is:

```
i = 5, l = 4
i = 5, l = 6
i = 4, l = 6
```

Because all functions must be called in the scope of a prototype, the compiler simply recognizes that fewer than the maximum number of arguments have been provided in the calls in cases 2 and 3, and it uses the default values from the function declaration.

When calling a function having default arguments, you must specify the leading part of the list. The declaration:

```
void test(int i = 4, long l);
```

is invalid, since the trailing arguments have no default value. That is, you cannot call this function using something like `test( , 10)`.

Consider the following prototype:

```
void print(const char *name = 0);
```

Default values are specified using an initializer-like format. In the case of `print`, you must

Default Argument Values

put a space or a formal parameter name between the * and =; otherwise, it will be incorrectly interpreted as the compound assignment operator *=.

A function can have default arguments and be overloaded at the same time, provided there are no ambiguities when the compiler tries to find a match for a call to that function.

Default argument information can accumulate by having multiple declarations of a function in the same scope. However, each successive redeclaration for the same function must add extra default argument information. For example:

```
/*1*/   void f(int i1     , int i2     , int i3     );
/*2*/   void f(int i1     , int i2     , int i3 = 1);
/*3*/   void f(int i1     , int i2     , int i3 = 1);    // error
/*4*/   void f(int i1     , int i2 = 0, int i3     );
/*5*/   void f(int i1 = 0, int i2     , int i3     );

void test()
{
        f();
}
```

Cases 2, 4, and 5[1] successively add more information to case 1. However, case 3 adds nothing to case 2, and so is rejected. The implication of this is that the exact same function declaration containing default argument information must not be seen by the compiler more than once in a compilation. Therefore, headers containing such function declarations must be protected appropriately against being processed more than once in the same compilation.

Default Arguments and Pointers to Functions

Thus far, we have looked only at calling functions directly by name. However, we may want to call functions indirectly via pointers. In such cases, can default arguments still be used effectively? The following example shows how:

```
#include <iostream.h>

void g(void (*pf)(int i1, int i2 = 4));
void f(int i1, int i2 = 4);

main()
{
        f(5);              // use default argument
        g(&f);

        return 0;
}
```

---
[1] Cases 4 and 5 are permitted because they provide additional information about function f. Either case on its own would otherwise be erroneous, as it is missing one or more trailing argument default values.

Any trailing function prototype argument may have a default value. And in the case of arguments that are themselves pointers to functions, the prototypes of their underlying functions may also contain default arguments, as in the case of function g above.

```
void g(void (*pf)(int i1, int i2 = 4))
{
        (*pf)(10, 20);          // don't use default argument
        (*pf)(30);              // use default argument
}
```

Like the corresponding prototype at the beginning of this example, this function definition also contains default argument information. This information is only permitted inside arguments that themselves contain prototypes; default arguments cannot otherwise exist here. For example, specifying a default value for the formal parameter `pf` itself is not allowed:

```
void f(int i1, int i2)
{
        cout << "i1 = " << i1 << ", i2 = " << i2 << '\n';
}
```

The output produced is:

```
i1 = 5, i2 = 4
i1 = 10, i2 = 20
i1 = 30, i2 = 4
```

Inline Functions

Introduction to Inlining

C++ has a keyword, `inline`, that permits functions to be "brought inline" each time they are called. This eliminates the overhead of calling the function and handling its return value, at the expense of making the executable code possibly larger. It is the old speed-versus-space trade-off we know so well in computing. (For some small functions, inlining them can reduce code size *and* improve performance!)

Like `register`, `inline` is a hint to the compiler. A compiler may decline to inline a function for a variety of reasons (for example, if it generates more than a certain amount of code or if it is recursive). Typically, there is no way to tell if an inline function has actually been inlined without looking at the generated code.

Taking the address of an `inline` function does not necessarily prevent it from being inlined; it could exist as a function as well as being inlined in one or more places.

Consider the case in which a function is declared inline and its definition is placed in a header. The header is included in 10 different source modules, each of which contains a call to the function. If the compiler decides, for whatever reason, not to actually inline the function, it must still accept the program as written. To do this, it must create a **static** version of that

Inline Functions

function in *each* module into which it is included. The end result is 10 identical, but private, copies of the same function in the one program.

Functions declared to be `inline` have internal linkage.

Consider the following example:

```
/* 1*/  // fn11.cpp
/* 2*/
/* 3*/  #include <iostream.h>
/* 4*/  #include "inline.h"
/* 5*/
/* 6*/  main()
/* 7*/  {
/* 8*/      f1(10);        // call inline function
/* 9*/      f2(10);        // call function-like macro
/*10*/
/*11*/      f1(20);        // call inline function
/*12*/      f2(20);        // call function-like macro
/*13*/
/*14*/      return 0;
/*15*/  }
```

where the header `inline.h` contains the following:

```
/* 1*/  // inline.h
/* 2*/
/* 3*/  inline void f1(int i)
/* 4*/  {
/* 5*/      cout << "i = " << i << " at line " << __LINE__
/* 6*/           << " in file " << __FILE__ << '\n';
/* 7*/  }
/* 8*/
/* 9*/  #define f2(i) cout << "i = " << i << " at line "         \
/*10*/                << __LINE__ << " in file " << __FILE__ << '\n';
```

The output produced is:

```
i = 10 at line 5 in file inline.h
i = 10 at line 9 in file fn11.cpp
i = 20 at line 5 in file inline.h
i = 20 at line 12 in file fn11.cpp
```

For the compiler to bring a function's code inline, the definition of the function must be in the same scope as the function calling it, since the compiler works on source files in isolation from each other. This is typically done by placing the function definition in a header.

When the inline function is actually brought inline, the values of the macros `__FILE__` and

__LINE__ correspond to their original source file values. The reason for this is that, unlike macros, inline functions are not expanded during preprocessing. However, with a function-like macro, __FILE__ and __LINE__ reflect the position at which the macro code was expanded.

C++ programmers prefer to use the inline function capability instead of function-like macros. The advantages of inline functions are that they can contain local declarations[2] and that type information is permitted and honored across function calls.

Enabling Inlining on a Selective Basis

It may be useful to organize your code so that you can switch inlining on or off for all or some functions, allowing you to measure the space/speed trade-off. The following example shows how to do this for all functions as a group:

```
// function.h

#ifdef INLINE
void swap(double *d1, double *d2)
{
        double temp;

        temp = *d1;
        *d1 = *d2;
        *d2 = temp;
}
#else
void swap(double *d1, double *d2);
#endif
```

By defining the macro INLINE before including this header, you bring in the inline versions. Similarly, this disables the noninline version in the user source file below:

```
// user.cpp

#include <iostream.h>
#include "function.h"

main()
{
        double a = 1.23, b = 5.67;
```

---

[2]Function-like macro definitions can also contain local declarations, but this can make them unwieldy and even unusable in certain circumstances.

Inline Functions

```
                cout << "a = " << a << ", b = " << b << '\n';
                swap(&a, &b);
                cout << "a = " << a << ", b = " << b << '\n';

                return 0;
        }
#ifndef INLINE
        void swap(double *d1, double *d2)
        {
                double temp;

                temp = *d1;
                *d1 = *d2;
                *d2 = temp;
        }
#endif
```

The output produced is:

```
a = 1.23, b = 5.67
a = 5.67, b = 1.23
```

To enable or disable inlining on a per-function basis, you would need a different macro for each function.

Some C++ compilers provide one or more compilation options to deal with inline functions. For example, you might be able to cause all `inline` keywords to be ignored. This could be useful during debugging, so the compiler can provide line number traceback. (Normally, traceback is not provided for inlined functions.) You might also be able to tell the compiler to inline functions beyond those explicitly labeled with `inline`, or you might be able to restrict it to just those explicitly labeled in that manner. However, you will not likely be able to control inlining on a per-function basis this way. For that, you have to revert to the conditional-compilation approach outlined above.

Chapter 3

Dynamic Memory Allocation

C++ provides an alternative way of allocating and freeing memory at run time using the keywords **new** and **delete**, respectively.

In this chapter, we will see how to allocate and free memory and how to trap memory allocation failures.

Introduction to Memory Allocation

The operator **new** is the equivalent of the function `malloc`. It also can emulate `calloc`. The operator **delete** is the equivalent of the function `free`. C++ does not, however, provide an equivalent of `realloc`.

Since **new** and **delete** are keywords (they are, in fact, operators), the compiler gets directly involved in generating the code to do the memory allocation.

In the following example, we will allocate memory for a **double**, an array of 20 **char**, and a structure of type **tag**:

```
#include <iostream.h>
#include <string.h>

struct tag {
        int i;
        double d;
        char *pch;
};

main()
{
        double *pd;
        char *pc;
        struct tag *pst, s = {10, 3.4, "abc"};
```

```
        // allocate memory for a scalar

/*1*/   pd = new double;
        if (pd == 0)
                cout << "pd allocation failure\n";
        else
                cout << "double allocated\n";

        // allocate memory for an array of 20 char

/*2*/   pc = new char [20];
        if (pc == 0)
                cout << "pc allocation failure\n";
        else {
                strcpy(pc, "Test message");
                cout << "string contains >" << pc << "<\n";
        }

        // allocate memory for a structure

/*3*/   pst = new tag;
        if (pst == 0)
                cout << "pst allocation failure\n";
        else {
                *pst = s;
                cout << "structure contains " << pst->i << ", "
                     << pst->d << ", " << pst->pch << '\n';
        }

        // free all allocated space

/*4*/   delete pd;
/*5*/   delete [] pc;
/*6*/   delete pst;

        return 0;
}
```

The output produced is:

```
double allocated
string contains >Test message<
structure contains 10, 3.4, abc
```

In case 1, the expression `pd = new double` requests that a `double` be allocated and its address be assigned to `pd`. This is equivalent to `pd = malloc(sizeof(double))`. And just as malloc and friends return a null pointer value on failure, so too does new. The initial value of the memory allocated by new is undefined.

In case 2, an array of 20 char is allocated and the address of the first element is stored in pc. Similarly, in case 3, pst = new tag causes pst to point to the allocated structure of type tag.

The delete operator is used to free up the allocated memory. Cases 4 and 6 are simple, since single objects are being freed. In case 5, we indicate that pc points to the first of an array of 20 char. It is undefined behavior if you omit the brackets when deleting an array or if you specify them when deleting a nonarray.

We have used delete even if the corresponding new failed. This is safe, because deleting a pointer containing the null pointer value causes no adverse behavior. In C, this results in undefined behavior.

Let's take a closer look at the allocation of arrays:

```
#include <iostream.h>

main()
{
        int n;
        double *pd;
        int (*pi)[5];

// allocate memory for a variable-size array of doubles

        n = 5;
/*1*/   pd = new double [n];
        if (pd == 0)
                cout << "pd allocation failure\n";

// allocate memory for an array of n x 5 ints

        n = 2;
/*2*/   pi = new int [n][5];
        if (pi == 0)
                cout << "pi #1 allocation failure\n";

        n = 0;
/*3*/   pi = new int [n][5];    // size = 0
        if (pi == 0)
                cout << "pi #2 allocation failure\n";

        return 0;
}
```

In case 1, new double [n] allows us to allocate a variable-sized array, something done often in C using `malloc` or `calloc`. In fact, only the first dimension is permitted to be nonconstant. In case 2, a two-dimensional array of size 2×5 is created since n is set to 2.

In case 3, we have `new int [n][5]` where n is set to zero. That is, we attempt to allocate a block of memory of size zero. C++ permits this, and the result is a non-null pointer. Subsequent allocations of zero bytes result in different non-null pointer values being returned[1].

When the two-dimensional arrays are allocated, a pointer to the first row is returned, and likewise for arrays of larger dimensions. And because each row is an array of 5 ints, pi must be declared as a pointer to an array of 5 int.

Because we have to declare the type of object we intend to store in the allocated space, the compiler can check attempts to misuse the allocated space. For example:

```
main()
{
        char *pc = new int;             // error

        int *pi = new int [10][5];      // error

        return 0;
}
```

Given that mixing C and C++ routines in the same program is feasible and, in many cases, desirable, you may ask, "Can I use `new/delete` and `malloc/free` in the same program?" The draft C++ standard states that the relationship between the two approaches to memory management is unspecified, so the answer is "Maybe."

Handling new Errors

A mechanism exists to trap `new` allocation failures by means other than checking for a null pointer. This method involves registering a user-written error handler. For example:

```
#include <iostream.h>
#include <stdlib.h>
#include <string.h>
#include <new.h>

void complain() // crude error handler
{
        cout << "new failed\n";

        exit(1);
}
```

---

[1] In Standard C, it is implementation-defined whether an allocation of zero bytes fails or succeeds with a non-null pointer being returned.

```
main()
{
        unsigned int n;
        char *pc1, *pc2;
        void (*old)();

        cout << "Enter array size: ";
        cin >> n;

        old = set_new_handler(complain);

        pc1 = new char[n];
        cout << "First array done\n";
        pc2 = new char[n];
        cout << "Second array done\n";

        delete pc1;
        delete pc2;

        return 0;
}
```

The error handler must take no arguments and have no return value. The registration function **set_new_handler** is declared in the header **new.h** and works much like **signal** in C, in that it registers a handler and at the same time gives you back the address of the previously registered handler so you can restore it in the future.

The idea of the error handler is to trap allocation failures in a manner that is transparent to the main code flow so you do not have to test for a null pointer at each usage of **new**.

At program start-up, no **new** error handler is registered. A registered error handler can be deregistered either by registering another function in its place or by calling **set_new_handler** with a null pointer argument.

C++ R3.0 provided machinery to handle exceptions. Once this approach is integrated into the C++ standard, and implementations start to support it more widely, it will become the preferred method of dealing with **new** allocation failures.

Chapter 4

References

C++ provides an aliasing mechanism, called a *reference*, separate from that provided by pointers. It is not intended to replace pointers but rather to augment them.

In this chapter, we will see how to use this mechanism to pass arguments to, and return values from, functions. We will also see how to apply it to variables in general. Finally, we will compare it to the aliasing mechanism provided by pointers.

Introduction to References

In C, we tend to talk about passing arguments *by value* or *by address*. We know that all objects except arrays can be passed by value, even structures and unions. In such cases, a private copy of the argument is passed to the called function (usually on a stack), and any changes to that local, private copy have no effect on the original object whose value was passed in.

Objects can also be passed by address. That is, their address (or in the case of arrays, structures, and unions, the address of their initial element or member) is passed to the called function. This function can, in the absence of the `const` qualifier on its formal parameters, indirectly modify the objects passed into it. When an address is being passed in, that address itself is passed by value. That is, a private copy of that address is pushed onto the stack so that it becomes an automatic pointer variable within that called function, just as an `int` argument is when passed by value.

Many people say that passing by address is the same as passing *by reference*, and we tend to use the terms interchangeably. This is not a problem in itself. However, if we look at the argument-passing mechanisms provided in other languages and the syntax used to access them, we find that these two terms perhaps ought to be kept separate. To demonstrate this, look at the following FORTRAN fragment. It does not matter whether you know FORTRAN or not; the example is simple and easy to follow:

```
    INTEGER I

    CALL CHANGE(I)
```

```
C Subroutine CHANGE alters its incoming argument

      SUBROUTINE CHANGE(A)
      INTEGER A

      A = 1

      RETURN

      END
```

In this example, subroutine CHANGE causes the value of the incoming integer variable I to be changed because that variable is passed in by reference, not by value. While passing by reference provides the same capability as passing by address, the former does not require explicit pointer notation. That is, FORTRAN need not have an address-of or dereference operator, since these operations are handled automatically by the compiler. On the other hand, languages that have explicit addressing operators also allow objects of address type. That is, they allow pointer variables.

FORTRAN supports passing by reference, and C passes by value or address. It so happens that C++ supports all three mechanisms. And since we can reasonably assume it uses the same notation as C for passing by value and by address, we can expect there to be some new notation to handle passing by reference.

Both FORTRAN and C++ simply treat an argument passed by reference to be an alias for the object originally passed in. *And the alias can be used in exactly the same context as the original variable name.* No special dereferencing notation is needed, so the notation is more natural, at least from a FORTRAN programmer's viewpoint. However, that is not true for C programmers who need to master explicit pointer notation anyway.

What then is the value of having references? First, references do not require explicit address notation and can provide some of the power of pointers without the related bugs. Second, you can create a reference variable that is an alias for an array element or a structure or union member. As such, it can be used to assign a simple name to one that would otherwise be more complicated. (For example, the name of a member in a nested structure would ordinarily require one or more dot operators.) This makes for cleaner library interfaces.

References can be quite useful. However, pointers provide much of the same capability, and C programmers need to be well-versed with pointers. In many cases, the use of pointers versus references will simply be a matter of style. One place references can be justified and are used a great deal, however, is in passing/returning large objects to/from functions, particularly in operator overloading functions, as we shall see in chapter 1, "Operator Overloading."

Passing Arguments by Reference

The following example contains three different versions of a simple add function: One expects arguments by value, one by address, and one by reference:

Passing Arguments by Reference

```
#include <iostream.h>

int add1(int i, int j);           // pass by value
int add2(int *pi, int *pj);       // pass by address
int add3(int &ri, int &rj);       // pass by reference
```

The new notation occurs in the prototype for add3[1]. This function expects two int arguments to be passed in by reference. The & punctuator is used to indicate "reference":

```
main()
{
        int a = 5, b = 10;

        cout << add1(a, b) << '\n';      // pass by value
        cout << add2(&a, &b) << '\n';    // pass by address
        cout << add3(a, b) << '\n';      // pass by reference

        return 0;
}
```

The calls to add1 and add3 are identical. The only difference is in the prototype, so without seeing or knowing what is in the prototype (it is often in a header), the reader cannot tell the difference. That is, it is not obvious how the argument is being passed. A C programmer would immediately assume the arguments were being passed by value, since no address-of operator & is present, and the arguments are not pointers:

```
int add1(int i, int j)
{
        return i + j;
}

int add2(int *pi, int *pj)
{
        return *pi + *pj;
}

int add3(int &ri, int &rj)
{
        return ri + rj;
}
```

---

[1] Many C++ programmers prefer to write the & up against the token that precedes it. If you also choose that approach, you must understand that the & actually applies only to the identifier following it. That is, in int& j = i, k;, j is a reference while k is an object, not a reference. It is this author's opinion that int &j = i, k; conveys this more clearly.

The output produced is:

```
15
15
15
```

The add3 function is defined just as its corresponding prototype implies, as you would expect. The primary difference between add2 and add3 is that in add2 the dereferencing is explicit, whereas in add3 it is implicit.

Because add2 and add3 are given addresses but have no business modifying the incoming arguments' values, it would have been prudent to have added const in their prototypes and definitions, as in:

```
int add2(const int *pi, const int *pj);
int add3(const int &ri, const int &rj);
```

This could also be done with add1 but would have no real value, since its arguments are passed in by value anyway.

An argument passed by reference without a const qualifier in the prototype can be modified from within the called function, as follows:

```
#include <iostream.h>

void add4(int i, int j, int *result);
void add5(int i, int j, int &result);

main()
{
        int a = 5, b = 10, result1, result2;

        add4(a, b, &result1);   /* call by address */
        add5(a, b, result2);    /* call by reference */

        cout << result1 << '\n';
        cout << result2 << '\n';

        return 0;
}

void add4(int i, int j, int *result)
{
        *result = i + j;
}
```

Passing Arguments by Reference

```
void add5(int i, int j, int &result)
{
        result = i + j;
}
```

The output produced is:

```
15
15
```

The functions `add4` and `add5` are quite similar. The only difference is that passing by reference allows the formal arguments to be used with a simpler, but not explicit, notation.

Some interesting questions arise when you pass an argument by reference. For example, what happens if the argument is a constant? What if the argument has a compatible but different type? Consider the following:

```
void f(int &i);

void test()
{
        int i;
        double d;

/*1*/   f(i);
/*2*/   f(5);           // error
/*3*/   f(i + 2);       // error
/*4*/   f(d);           // error
}
```

Case 1 is the only acceptable one. When an argument is passed by reference, the compiler assumes that argument will be modified within the called function. Cases 2 and 3 involve a constant and a temporary value, respectively, while case 4 involves an object of a different type. In these three cases, it makes no sense to let function `f` modify the incoming argument, since it does not designate an `int` object.

The invalid calls will be accepted, however, if the prototype contains the `const` qualifier, as follows:

```
void f(const int &i);
```

Now, the compiler creates a temporary variable of type `int`, initializes it with the value of the argument given, and passes the temporary by reference. Since the incoming argument to `f` is now a reference to a `const`-qualified object, that object cannot be modified within `f`.

A function may be overloaded as long as each version of it has a unique signature. For this reason, the following two prototypes are not permitted in the same scope:

```
void f(int &ri);         // pass int by reference
void f(int i);           // pass int by value
```

The compiler sees we intend to call the two functions differently, but in each case the actual types of the arguments are the same. All that is different is that in one case the compiler passes by value and in the other it implicitly generates a reference and passes that. The calls to these functions are identical, and so the compiler cannot distinguish between them.

A reference is not quite a "full" type but rather is an aliasing mechanism, and one that is subtly different from that provided by pointers.

Functions that Return References

A function may return a reference. The following example shows two versions of the same function: One returns a char by reference, the other, a char by address:

```
#include <iostream.h>

char &f1(int i);         // return reference
char *f2(int i);         // return address

main()
{
        char c;

        f1(1) = 'A';
        f1(3) = 'B';
        f1(5) = 'C';
        f1(0);           // ignore return value

        *f2(1) = 'A';
        *f2(3) = 'B';
        *f2(5) = 'C';
        f2(0);           // ignore return value

        return 0;
}
char &f1(int i)
{
        static char str1[] = "_____";

        cout << "str1 = " << str1 << '\n';

        return str1[i];      // return reference
}
```

```
char *f2(int i)
{
        static char str2[] = "_____";

        cout << "str2 = " << str2 << '\n';

        return &str2[i];        // return address
}
```

The output produced is:

```
str1 = _____
str1 = _A_____
str1 = _A_B___
str1 = _A_B_C_
str2 = _____
str2 = _A_____
str2 = _A_B___
str2 = _A_B_C_
```

Again, the reference approach has a slightly simpler notation. However, this syntax is not intuitive to C programmers. When C programmers see an expression such as:

```
f1(1) = 'A'
```

they should immediately become suspicious. In C, the function call operator never produces an lvalue and, therefore, can never be the direct object of an assignment (or ++ or --) operator. For such a construct to exist in C, `f1` would have to be a macro that expanded not only to an lvalue but to one that was also modifiable. And writing a macro in this way would be very bad style. On the other hand, the pointer version:

```
*f2(1) = 'A'
```

is overt and very intuitive to C programmers. As we can see, in C++ the function call operator can produce a modifiable lvalue, but only if the function is returning a reference.

Of course, returning a local variable by reference has the same implications as does returning a local variable's address. If the local variable has automatic storage duration, it no longer exists when the calling function actually regains control. Therefore, `str1` and `str2` are static variables.

References Outside Function Calls

Thus far, we have talked about references only in the context of a function call. However, C++ permits this aliasing mechanism in other contexts, as well. For example, you can create a named alias for an object without ever calling a function. For example:

```
#include <iostream.h>

void f1(int *pi);
void f2(int &pi);

main()
{
        int i;
        int &ri = i;

        i = 5;          /* modify i directly */
        cout << "i = " << i << '\n';

        f1(&i);         /* modify i via pointer */
        cout << "i = " << i << '\n';

        ri = 10;        /* modify i via reference ri */
        cout << "i = " << i << '\n';

        f2(i);          /* modify i via reference */
        cout << "i = " << i << '\n';

        f2(ri);         /* modify i via reference ri */
        cout << "i = " << i << '\n';

        return 0;
}
```

The declaration int &ri = i declares that ri is an alias to the variable i. ri is not a variable in its own right, but simply an alias for another variable. Any context that permits the name i to be used also permits ri, with exactly the same results. You can modify i directly by assignment and indirectly by passing its address to f1. You can also modified i directly through its reference alias ri, by passing i directly by reference to f2, or by passing its reference alias ri to f2.

When a reference such as ri is declared, it must have an initializer, and that reference remains aliased to the object identified in its initializer. Unlike pointers, named references cannot be made to alias different objects at different times during program execution.

Consider the following example:

```
void f1(int *pi)
{
        *pi = 777;
}
```

```
void f2(int &i)
{
        i = 987;
}
```

The output produced is:

```
i = 5
i = 777
i = 10
i = 987
i = 987
```

This example demonstrates that C++ departs subtly from C with regard to assignment. In C, numerous things are defined in terms of assignment, such as ++ and -- operators, passing arguments, and returning values from functions. Initializers for automatic scalars are treated just like assignments. That is, `int i = 5;` is equivalent to `int i; i = 5;`. This is not true with references in C++. For example, consider the following:

```
int i;
int &ri = i;

ri = i;
```

The initializer indicates that `ri` is an alias for `i`. However, the assignment says to assign the value of the variable `i` to the object being aliased by `ri`. Effectively, this assigns `i` to itself. The two are treated quite differently. When arguments are passed or returned by reference, they behave just like the initializer above, not like the assignment.

Earlier we saw that there were limits on the kinds of expressions that can be passed by reference. Specifically, if the expression does not designate an object, it cannot be passed by reference unless the `const` qualifier is used. A similar situation occurs with local references. For example:

```
/*1*/   int &ri1 = 123;         // error
/*2*/   const int &ri2 = 123;   // OK
```

`ri1` cannot be a reference to a constant. The only way to create such a reference is if the `const` qualifier is applied, as in case 2.

Here is another example showing that an alias is permitted anywhere in place of the object to which it is aliased:

```
void f1(int i);
void f2(int &ri);
```

```
main()
{
        int i = 10;
        int &ri = i;

        f1(i);
        f1(ri);
        f2(i);
        f2(ri);

        return 0;
}
```

In the case of the calls to f1, i is passed by value using its name and then by value using the name of its alias. With f2, i is passed by reference using its name and using the name of its reference. That is, passing a reference by reference is the same as passing the aliased object by reference. On the basis of your experience with pointers, you might expect an extra level of indirection is being generated here, but that is not the case. A reference to a reference to a reference, and so on, is the same as a reference to the original object itself. For example, consider the following declarations:

```
int i = 10;      // original object
int &r1 = i;     // alias for i
int &r2 = i;     // alias for i
int &r3 = r1;    // alias for r1 and i
```

Of course, references can be created as aliases for pointers too. For example:

```
#include <iostream.h>

void f(int * &rpi);

main()
{
        int i = 10;
        int *pi = &i;
        int *&rpi = pi;

        cout << "*pi  = " << *pi << '\n';
        cout << "*rpi = " << *rpi << '\n';

/*1*/   f(pi);
/*2*/   f(rpi);
```

References Outside Function Calls

```
                cout << "*pi = " << *pi << '\n';
                cout << "*rpi = " << *rpi << '\n';

                return 0;
        }
        void f(int * &rpi)
        {
                static int j = 123;

                rpi = &j;
        }
```

The output produced is:

```
*pi  = 10
*rpi = 10
*pi  = 123
*rpi = 123
```

In case 1, the pointer `pi` is passed by reference, whereas in case 2, a reference to that pointer is passed by reference. In either case, the pointer can be modified from within f itself.

References can also be aliases for array elements, structure members, or union members. For example:

```
#include <iostream.h>

main()
{
        int i[] = {9, 8, 7, 6};
        int &ri = i[2];
        int &rj = i[3];

        cout << "ri = " << ri << ", rj = " << rj << '\n';

        struct {
                int i;
                double d;
                unsigned bf : 3;
        } s = {10, 1.23, 5};

        union {
                int i;
                double d;
        } u = {123};
```

```
                int &rk = s.i;
                int &rl = u.i;
//              unsigned int &rm = s.bf;        // error

                double &rd1 = s.d;
                double &rd2 = u.d;

                cout << "s.i = " << rk << ", s.d = " << rd1 << '\n';
                cout << "u.i = " << rl;
                rd2 = 987.654;
                cout << ", u.d = " << rd2 << '\n';

                return 0;
        }
```

The output produced is:

```
ri = 7, rj = 6
s.i = 10, s.d = 1.23
u.i = 123, u.d = 987.654
```

In the case of **unsigned int &rm = s.bf;**, we are attempting to create a reference to a bit-field. Since bit-fields are not addressable, this is invalid. In a similar vein, a bit-field cannot be passed directly by reference, even if the widened type of the bit-field matches that in the function's prototype.

Ordinarily, a reference cannot be made to alias something other than that to which it is initialized. Consider the following example:

```
void f(int index)
{
        static char text[] = "ABC";
        char &c = text[index];

        cout << "text[" << index << "] = " << c << '\n';
}
```

c is an alias for an unknown element of array **text**. And since the function **f** can be called with different values for **index**, **c** can be used as an alias for any of the elements, but only one at a time.

A reference type can be hidden inside a **typedef**, as follows:

```
typedef int &ri;

int i = 10;
ri x = i;
```

A reference can also have **extern** storage class. For example:

```
// source file 1

int i = 123;
int &er = i;

// source file 2

extern int &er; // extern reference
```

In such cases, the aliases created by references must be maintained beyond compilation, since an **extern** reference can be resolved only at link time. In this case, the reference does not need an initializer. The object to which it refers is determined at link time.

An expression may be explicitly cast into a reference type. Such casts produce an lvalue, while all other casts do not.

References Versus Pointers

While a reference is somewhat like a pointer, a pointer is an object that occupies memory and has an address. Non-**const** pointers can also be made to point to different objects at run time. On the other hand, a reference is an alias for an object and does not, itself, occupy any memory. Its address and value are the address and value of the object to which it is aliased. And while you can have a reference to a pointer, you cannot have a pointer to a reference or an array of references, nor can you have an object of some reference type. References to the **void** type are also prohibited.

References and pointers are not interchangeable. A reference to an **int** cannot, for example, be assigned to a pointer to an **int**, or vice versa. However, a reference to a pointer to an **int** can be assigned a pointer to an **int**.

Part II

Using Existing Class Libraries

Chapter 5

Standard Class Libraries

Many people believe that programmers must understand a great deal about object-oriented programming to get real work done with C++. This need not be the case at all. If C++ programmers have access to a variety of tested, robust, and well-documented class libraries, they can deal with these libraries as though they were "black boxes." The fact that these libraries might use object-oriented programming in their implementation might be interesting. However, that is the business of the people implementing and/or maintaining these libraries. All that users of those libraries need do is to read the functional description of the modules in the library and to use them on the basis of their published interface.

Apart from the Standard C library, the only other library guaranteed to be present in a C++ implementation is that for doing I/O. In this chapter, we will discuss two other commonly supplied libraries that support string manipulation and complex numbers.

Introduction to Classes

In C++, libraries are centered around classes. Simply stated, a *class* is just another name for a structure. The I/O class library consists of a series of headers and object libraries. The headers contain structure type definitions and function prototypes. They also may contain macros, **const** object definitions, and inline versions of some functions.

Apart from the standard I/O class, implementations often include a number of class libraries such as complex numbers, packed-decimal arithmetic, string processing, support for various types of lists (such as linked lists and binary trees), vectors, and matrices. There is also a growing number of classes becoming available from commercial third-party sources. One area of high activity involves support for windowing.

The whole purpose behind a class is to hide the implementation details from the end user. This allows you to change or enhance those details without affecting existing code.

Consider the type **FILE** defined in Standard C. Does a C programmer need to know what a **FILE** object really is to be able to use it effectively? Of course not. This type is an abstract data type. We are told enough about it so we can use it. However, we need know nothing about how it works. If you look in most versions of **stdio.h**, you will see something such as the following:

```
typedef struct {
        /* implementation details go here */
} FILE;
```

On the basis of this definition, we can declare objects of type `FILE`, as well as pointers to and arrays of, such objects. We also can assign one `FILE` or `FILE` pointer to another. We really don't think twice about what is going on behind the scenes when we declare a `FILE` pointer and initialize it with the valued returned from `fopen`. The same applies to class libraries in C++.

C++ contains machinery to program using an object-oriented approach. This is useful and is utilized in designing and implementing the class libraries themselves. Certainly, many C++ programmers who start out using classes designed by others will be interested in designing classes of their own. However, designing nontrivial classes requires a lot of experience in both C++ and OOP techniques. And just like object libraries in any other language, you do not want everyone on a project implementing them. In fact, you probably want a select few people working on them.

One of the big promises of C++ is code reuse. This is achieved primarily by proper class design and the ability to use that class in future projects. And as needs change and projects evolve, new classes can be derived from existing classes, thereby preserving the investment in code and programmers. However, these benefits are not controlled by the "rank and file" C++ programmer; they are a direct reflection on the work of the class designer.

We now will look at the string and complex class libraries, not so much to learn how to use these classes in particular, but to see how to use class libraries in general.

String Manipulation

Not all C++ implementations provide a string class library. And in those that do, the string classes may differ in certain subtle, and not so subtle, ways. The string class described in this section is based on a common subset of various implementations. It is presented here so we can see an example of how to interpret the interface documentation for a class.

General Description

The C++ library includes the Standard C header `string.h`. This header declares a family of functions that allow strings to be manipulated. For example, they can be copied, compared, concatenated, and searched. A string is represented as null-terminated arrays of `char`s. We will refer to an object of this type by the name *string*.

Now while we can do useful string manipulation with this family of functions, the notation we use is quite different from that we use with built-in types. For example, we cannot assign strings directly. Instead, we must call `strcpy`. Similarly, we cannot use the relational or equality operators on strings; the array names get converted to pointers immediately, and we must use `strcmp` instead. And to concatenate strings, we must use `strcat` instead of the more intuitive addition operator.

The C++ string library allows us to deal with character strings as first-class objects. That is, we can treat them just like built-in types. We can use the operators we already know, such as =, >, <=, and +, in a meaningful way with strings. A string that can be manipulated in this manner will be referred to by the name *String*. A String simply is some way of packaging a string so it can be manipulated as a whole.

Parent Header

Each class is described in a corresponding header, and a header may contain multiple class definitions. For the purpose of this discussion, let us call the string class header **strings.h**[1].

This header will define the class type itself. We use this type just as we use typedef names in C. For example:

```
#include <strings.h>

String s1;                    // global String

String *test(String s2)
{
        static String s3;     // block-scope static String
        String s4[5];         // block-scope auto array of 5 Strings

        return &s3;
}
```

A String is an object. Therefore, we can can create instances of that object type, pointers to Strings, and arrays of Strings. We can have Strings as members of structures and unions and we can pass them to functions and return them from functions by value, address, or reference. In short, a String can be used syntactically in the same way as a built-in nonarray type.

Constructors and Destructors

In the example above, we have avoided the question of initialization. Ordinarily, we could initialize a structure by providing a comma-separated brace-delimited initializer list. However, that requires us to know the number of members, their order, and whether or not they are contained inside nested structures. Since the internal representation of a class object is intended to be hidden, we need some other way of initializing user-defined objects.

The approach we use involves constructors. A *constructor* is a special function that is called automatically each time an object of the class is created. This guarantees that each object starts out its life in a predictable state. One or more constructors will be provided as part of the class library. Consider the following constructors for class **String**:

```
String(const char *pstr = "");
String(const String &Str);
```

---

[1] The actual name varies from one implementation to another; some use **String.h**, while others use **strng.h** or **string.hxx**. Standard C++ will most likely include a string class. If that is the case, that class will eventually have a standard name.

The first things to note are that these are overloaded versions of the same function and that the function is named the same as its class. That is what distinguishes it as a constructor.

Each function takes one argument. In the first case, a `const char` is expected to be passed by address, and if no argument is supplied, a pointer to a null string will be used as the default argument. In the second case, a `const String` is expected, and it will be passed by reference. Remember that overloaded functions can also have default arguments, provided a call to these functions is not ambiguous.

The following example makes both implicit and explicit use of these constructors:

```
#include <strings.h>

char name[] = "Mary";

String s1;
String s2("hello");
String s3 = "hello";
static String s4(name);
String s5(s3);

main()
{
        String s6 = s3;
        String s7[][2] = {
                {"Tom", s4},
                {s5, "Kathleen"}
        };

        String *ps1 = new String;
        String *ps2 = new String("abc");
        String *ps3 = new String [5];

        delete ps1;
        delete ps2;
        delete [] ps3;

        return 0;
}
```

In C, objects having static storage duration and no initializer take on an initial value of zero cast to their type. In the case of structures or arrays, zero is cast to the type of each member or element. Objects having automatic storage duration and no initializer take on some undefined value. These rules also apply to C++ for nonclass objects.

In the example above, s1 is initialized to a null string. That is, in the absence of an explicit initializer, the *default constructor* is called to initialize this object. The default constructor is that constructor either having no arguments or having default values for all arguments.

String Manipulation 53

The definition of **s2** has what appears to be an argument list following it. And that is what it is—an argument list to a constructor. The compiler uses this information to determine which constructor is to be called to initialize that object.

The initializers for **s2** and **s3** represent alternate ways of saying the same thing.

Like **s2**, **s4** takes an array of characters as its initializer argument. This is more powerful than C, which requires that static variables such as **s3** be initialized only with compile-time constant expressions.

s5 is initialized using the second constructor, as is **s6**. **s7** is a two-dimensional array of strings initialized as shown.

When **new** is used to allocate memory for a class object, the appropriate constructor is also called. In the case of **ps1**, the String allocated contains a null string, while in the case of **ps2**, it is the string **abc**. The only restriction with **new** is that when it is used to allocate memory for an array, a constructor cannot be called explicitly; the default constructor is always used.

A *destructor* is another special function. It is called each time a class object goes out of scope. If a destructor has been designed properly, you never need to know of its existence.

While a constructor can be called to perform initialization, it is often called directly. For example:

```
#include <strings.h>

void change_String(const String &old_String, const String &new_String);

String get_String()
{
/*1*/   change_String(String("Red"), String("Blue"));

/*2*/   return String("Green");
}
```

In case 1, the function **change_String** is called, and two Strings are passed by reference. However, the actual arguments are not named objects. Instead, they are unnamed temporary Strings that have been created specifically for this function call. They are created, then passed by reference to the function, and then deleted. Their life is over by the end of their parent expression.

In case 2, another unnamed temporary String is created. A copy of it is returned by the function **get_String**, and the temporary is deleted.

These uses of constructors effectively allow us to create a structure constant.

Operator Functions

One of the benefits of dealing with class objects as if they were built-in types is that we can perform I/O on them directly, using the same machinery. For example:

```
#include <iostream.h>
#include <strings.h>

main()
{
        String s1("Hello");
        String s2;

        cout << "Enter a string: ";
        cin >> s2;
        cout << "|" << s1 << "|" << s2 << "|\n";

        return 0;
}
```

The output produced is:

```
Enter a string: Friday
|Hello|Friday|
```

The user documentation will contain operator function declarations similar to the following prototypes:

```
friend ostream &operator<<(ostream &os, const String &Str);
friend istream &operator>>(istream &is, String &Str);
```

These simply say that the I/O operators have been overloaded to handle Strings. We can ignore the details of these declarations.

A number of other operations also will be defined for this class. For example, equality of strings often is declared as follows:

```
friend int operator==(const String &Str1, const String &Str2);
friend int operator==(const String &Str, const char *);
friend int operator==(const char *, const String &Str);
```

The first function declaration indicates that two Strings can be compared using the equality operator ==. The second function declaration indicates that a String can be compared directly with a string. However, the String must be the left operand. The third function declaration indicates that a string can be compared with a String. In this case, the String must be the right operand. An example of using all three forms of equality follows:

```
String s1("Top");
String s2("Bottom");

if (s1 == s2 || s1 == "Down" || "Bottom" == s2)
        // ...
```

The equality operator functions return `int`, just as the built-in version of that operator returns an `int`. And if the comparison is false, a value of zero is returned, while true is represented by a value of 1. This demonstrates an important property of a well-designed class. The operators defined for that class should behave in an intuitive manner on the basis of the user's knowledge of built-in types.

There will be three corresponding operator functions for each of the operators !=, <, <=, >, and >=. There also will be operator functions for concatenating two Strings or a String and a string. For example:

```
friend String operator+(const String &Str1, const String &Str2);
friend String operator+(const String &Str, const char *);
friend String operator+(const char *, const String &Str);
```

These can be used in the obvious way, as follows:

```
String s1("X");
String s2("Y");
String s3;

s3 = s2 + "abc" + ("xyz" + s3);
```

The operator functions declared thus far are for binary operators, and both operands have been declared explicitly. This has been indicated by the use of the keyword `friend`. It is possible that any or all of the preceding operator functions are declared a little differently than shown here. If the keyword `friend` is missing, the left operand will be missing from the function declaration and is automatically assumed to be of the class type. For example, assignment might be declared as follows:

```
String &operator=(const String &Str);
String &operator=(const char *pstr);

String &operator+=(const String &Str);
String &operator+=(const char *);
```

These functions declare that a String can have assigned, or concatenated to it another String or a string.

Member Functions

There are a number of other useful operations we might wish to perform on a String. For example, we might want capabilities equivalent to C's `strchr`, `strrchr`, `strstr`, and `strlen` functions. We can do these things as long as the class includes the corresponding *member functions*. Consider the declarations of the following member functions for class `String`:

```
unsigned Strlen() const;
String   upper() const;
String   lower() const;
```

These functions are called by name. However, because they are specific to the class **String**, the notation we use to call them is different than for functions in C. For example:

```
#include <iostream.h>
#include <strings.h>

main()
{
        String s("Hello");
        String *ps = &s;

        cout << "s: " << s
             << ", length = " << s.Strlen()
             << ", lowercase = " << s.lower()
             << ", uppercase = " << ps->upper() << "\n";

        return 0;
}
```

The output produced is:

```
s: Hello, length = 5, lowercase = hello, uppercase = HELLO
```

The three functions are called using **s.Strlen()**, **s.lower()**, and **ps->upper()**. The reason for this is these functions are members of the class **String**, and as such, we use the member selection dot operator in the first two cases and the member selection arrow operator in the third case.

The case-conversion functions return converted copies of their input Strings; they do not modify the input Strings directly.

Complex Numbers

Quite a few C++ implementations provide a class library that is capable of representing and manipulating complex numbers. In this section, we will look at the user interface for this class.

General Description

A complex number consists of two parts: real and imaginary. Various operations are defined for complex numbers. For example, they can be added, subtracted, multiplied, and so forth, with other complex or real numbers. They also can be passed to various transcendental and hyperbolic math functions, and they can be input and output.

Complex Numbers

Parent Header

The complex class header is `complex.h`. It contains a definition of the class type itself, along with all the necessary support machinery.

Constructors and Destructors

Two constructors are usually provided. They are:

```
complex(double real, double imaginary = 0);
complex();
```

The first accepts either one or two arguments, with the second defaulting to an imaginary part of zero. The default constructor initializes the real and imaginary parts to zero.

There is no destructor.

Operator Functions

Complex numbers can be read and written using the following I/O operator functions:

```
ostream &operator<<(ostream &os, const complex &z);
istream &operator>>(istream &is, complex &z);
```

The binary arithmetic operators +, -, *, and / are provided, as are the unary arithmetic operators + and - and the comparison operators == and !=. For example:

```
friend complex operator+(const complex &z1, const complex &z2);
friend complex operator+(double d, const complex &z);
friend complex operator+(const complex &z, double d);
```

```
complex operator-();
```

```
friend int operator==(const complex &z1, const complex &z2);
friend int operator!=(const complex &z1, const complex &z2);
```

Member Functions

Some of the math member functions are:

```
friend complex cos(complex &z);
friend complex cosh(complex &z);
```

```
friend complex pow(const complex &base, double exponent);
friend complex pow(double base, const complex &exponent);
friend complex pow(const complex &base, const complex &exponent);
```

The three versions of the power function provide for the three possible combinations of base and exponent: a complex number raised to a real power, a real number raised to a complex power, and a complex number raised to a complex power.

Complex Example

The following example demonstrates the use of a number of the constructor, operator, and member functions of the complex class:

```
#include <complex.h>
#include <iostream.h>

main()
{
        complex z1;
        complex z2(0.15, -0.6);
        complex z3(0.5, 0.1);

        cout << "z1 = " << z1 << '\n';
        cout << "z2 = " << z2 << '\n';

        cout << "real(z3) = " << real(z3) << '\n';
        cout << "imag(z3) = " << imag(z3) << '\n';

        z1 += -z2 + complex(1.5, 3.1) - 0.1;

        cout << "z1 = " << z1 << '\n';

        cout << ((z2 == z3) ? "z2 == z3" : "z2 != z3") << '\n';

        return 0;
}
```

The output produced is:

```
z1 = (0, 0)
z2 = (0.15, -0.6)
real(z3) = 0.5
imag(z3) = 0.1
z1 = (1.25, 3.7)
z2 != z3
```

Chapter 6

Input and Output

C++ has an alternate way of performing I/O, primarily by using the header `iostream.h`. Why have an alternate way to perform I/O? There are two reasons: to "fix" some of the problems inherent with the I/O in C, and to provide a way to handle user-defined types.

In this chapter, we will see how to use `cout` and `cin` to achieve the same effect as if we had used `printf` and `scanf`. We will also see how to do file I/O and how to format into, and decode from, strings.

Format Control

cout, as well as `cerr` and `clog`, uses some default output formatting. For example:

```
#include <iostream.h>
#include <ctype.h>

main()
{
        static char ca[] = "text";
        char *pc = ca;

/*1*/   cout << "x = " << tolower('X') << " " << (char)tolower('X') << "\n";
/*2*/   cout << "ca = " << ca << " pc = " << pc << "\n";
/*3*/   cout << "&pc = " << &pc << "\n"
             << "&ca[0] = " << (void *)ca << "\n";

        return 0;
}
```

The output produced is:

```
x = 120 x
ca = text pc = text
&pc = 0xcfbfff4
&ca[0] = 0xcfb00aa
```

In case 1, integer values are output as decimal, except for those of type `char`, which are written instead as characters. Only the significant digits are displayed by default.

In case 2, we see that a pointer to `char` is like the `%s` specifier in `printf`. The address of a null-terminated character string is expected, which results in that string's being printed.

In case 3, there is an explicit `void *` cast. If the right operand of `<<` is a pointer of type other than "pointer to `char`," the address is output in an implementation-defined format just like `printf`'s `%p` specifier. To output the address of the first character, we must cast explicitly to a `void` pointer, instead, as shown.

You can override the defaults used by `<<`. For example, the following program displays numbers in octal and hexadecimal bases, as well as decimal, in right-justified columns:

```
#include <iostream.h>
#include <iomanip.h>

main()
{
        int i;

        cout << " char    dec    oct    hex\n";
        for (i = 'A'; i <= 'F'; ++i)
                cout << setw(4) << (char)(i)
                     << setw(7) << dec << i
                     << setw(7) << oct << i
                     << setw(7) << hex << i << "\n";

        return 0;
}
```

The output produced is:

```
 char   dec    oct    hex
   A     65    101     41
   B     66    102     42
   C     67    103     43
   D     68    104     44
   E     69    105     45
   F     70    106     46
```

The identifiers `dec`, `oct`, `hex`, and `setw` are used to provide behavior like some of `printf`'s conversion specifiers. Such directives are called *manipulators*. While these identifiers are not keywords, they have special meaning in the context of input and/or output constructs. In fact,

Format Control

each causes a corresponding library function to be called, which changes the state of the specified stream as requested. The manipulators `dec`, `oct`, and `hex` have no arguments and are defined in `iostream.h`. A number of other manipulators are also defined there. The complete set is:

Manipulators Having No Arguments

Manipulator	Purpose
dec	Sets the stream's radix to decimal.
endl	Inserts a new-line and flushes the stream (output only).
ends	Inserts a null character (output only).
flush	Flushes the stream (output only).
hex	Sets the stream's radix to hexadecimal.
oct	Sets the stream's radix to octal.
ws	Skips white space (input only).

By default, output streams are buffered, so use `flush` or `endl` to write out immediately. Manipulators that take a single argument, such as `setw`, are defined in `iomanip.h`. This set consists of:

Manipulators Having One Argument

Manipulator	Purpose
resetiosflags	Clears format state flags (see below).
setbase	Sets number base to 0, 8, 10, or 16.
setfill	Sets fill character.
setiosflags	Sets format state flags (see below).
setprecision	Sets precision.
setw	Sets field width.

The default width for each field is exactly the number of print positions needed, so we have to put the `setw` manipulator before all three output values. By using `setw` on an input stream, we can limit the number of characters read when reading in a string, just as the width field can be used with `scanf`'s `%s` specifier.

The effect of all manipulators except `setw` persists beyond the I/O field that they precede. For example:

```
#include <iostream.h>

main()
{
        int i = 20;
```

```
/*1*/    cout << hex << i << " " << 2 * i << '\n';
/*2*/    cout << i << '\n';
/*3*/    cout << dec << i << '\n';

         return 0;
}
```

The output produced is:

```
14 28
14
20
```

setw is the only manipulator whose effect is reset after each input or output operation.

In many programs, I/O is interleaved on the same stream from multiple functions. In such cases, each function performing I/O should leave each stream it uses in a predictable state. Consider the following example:

```
#include <iostream.h>

void display();

main()
{
        int i = 20;

        cout << "i = " << i << '\n';
        display();
        cout << "i = " << i << '\n';

        return 0;
}
void display()
{
        cout << hex << 100 << '\n';
}
```

The output produced is:

```
i = 20
64
i = 14
```

Both output statements in main appear to do exactly the same thing. However, as we see, function display permanently changes the output stream mode from decimal to hexadecimal.

Format Control 63

It should, instead, restore the stream to its original state, as follows:

```
void display()
{
        long flag_status = cout.flags();

        cout << hex << 100 << '\n';
        cout.flags(flag_status);
}
```

Now the output produced is:

```
i = 20
64
i = 20
```

As shown, the member function `flags` can be used both to get and to set a stream's state. When it is used to set a new state, it returns the current state.

The single-purpose manipulators cater to only some of the formatting you might require, such as precision and width. They do not provide for left or right justification, forcing leading plus sign, floating-point format, or the various alternate output forms permitted with `printf`'s flags. To achieve these things, we must use the pair of general-purpose manipulators, `setiosflags` and `resetiosflags`.

Each open stream maintains a series of bit-flags. Each flag records whether a particular attribute is or is not set. This set of flags records the stream's *format state*. In `iostream.h`, an enumerated type is defined with a set of enumeration constant names for each format state. The set of enumeration constants is as follows:

Format State Flags

Name	Purpose
dec	Decimal conversion.
fixed	Uses f-style floating notation.
hex	Hexadecimal conversion.
internal	Padding after sign or base indicator.
left	Left-justify output.
oct	Octal conversion.
right	Right-justify output.
scientific	Uses e-style floating notation.
showbase	Uses base indicator on output.

Format State Flags (continued)

Name	Purpose
showpoint	Forces decimal point (floating output).
showpos	Adds leading + to positive integers.
skipws	Skips white space on input.
stdio	Flushes `stdout`, `stderr` after insertion.
unitbuf	Flushes all streams after insertion.
uppercase	Uppercase hex output or exponent.

Because each enumeration constant is a power of 2, you can OR them together to set or clear more than one flag at a time[1] . An example of the use of these enumeration constants follows:

```
#include <iostream.h>
#include <iomanip.h>

main()
{
/*1*/   cout << 123 << hex << setw(8) << setfill('*') << 123 << '\n';
/*2*/   cout << setprecision(3) << 1.23789 << '\n';
/*3*/   cout << resetiosflags(ios::hex) << 123 << '\n';
/*4*/   cout << setw(10) << setiosflags(ios::right) << "abcd" << '\n';

        return 0;
}
```

The output produced is:

```
123******7b
1.238
123
******abcd
```

The enumeration constant names are defined inside the predefined class type `ios`, so to refer to them we must qualify them with their parent class name `ios::`, as shown.

Stream Member Functions

The screen and keyboard I/O streams are not special; they are of the same type as those established with files. Thus far, we have accessed these standard streams using only the insertion and extraction operators. However, the library provides an equivalent set of member functions to perform equivalent operations. For example:

---

[1]The standard stream member functions `setf` and `unsetf` can also be used to set and to clear bit-flags, respectively.

```
#include <iostream.h>

main()
{
        char c;

        while ((c = cin.get()) != EOF)
                cout.put(c);

        return 0;
}
```

The output produced is:

```
This is a test.<return>
This is a test.
<eof>
```

The function `get`, one version of which behaves like C's `getchar`, is defined as a member function of class `istream`, while `put`, one version of which behaves like C's `putchar`, is a member function of class `ostream`. Therefore, `get` and `put` can be called for the standard I/O streams as well as any other explicitly opened files.

We can read in a whole string using `getline`, as follows:

```
#include <iostream.h>

main()
{
        char text[11];

        cout << "Enter text (10 chars max): ";
        cin.getline(text, 11);
        cout << "text = |" << text << "|\n";

        cout << "Enter text (10 chars max): ";
        cin.getline(text, 11, ' ');
        cout << "text = |" << text << "|\n";

        cout << "Enter text (10 chars max): ";
        cin.getline(text, 11);
        cout << "text = |" << text << "|\n";

        return 0;
}
```

The function `getline` behaves like C's `fgets` function. It takes three arguments: The first is the destination of the read; the second is the maximum length to be read; and the third is the character to be used to terminate the read if fewer than the maximum number of characters is input. A null character is appended to the string read. If the terminating character argument is omitted, '\n' is used by default. If present in the input, the terminating character is not stored in the string; it is discarded.

Some input and its corresponding output are:

```
Enter text (10 chars max): 12345
text = |12345|
Enter text (10 chars max): a b
text = |a|
Enter text (10 chars max): text = |b|
```

Because the first string is less than 11 characters, the new-line terminates it and is discarded. The space character in the next input separates it into two strings:

```
Enter text (10 chars max): 1234567890
text = |1234567890|
Enter text (10 chars max): a b
text = |
a|
Enter text (10 chars max): text = |b|
```

The first string contains 10 characters, and along with the trailing null character, this fills the destination array. The new-line entered is beyond this input and remains in the input stream. In fact, it becomes the first character read and retained in the second string, as shown.

There is also a version of **get** that takes the same three arguments as **getline**. The only difference is that **get** leaves the terminating character in the input stream for the next read.

The set of member functions for performing I/O are listed below:

I/O Member Functions

Function	Purpose
gcount()	Reports the number of characters read.
get()	Reads a character (like C's `getchar` and `fgetc`).
getline(char *, int, char)	Reads a string (like C's `fgets`).
ignore(int, int)	Reads and ignores characters.
peek()	Gets a character without actually reading it.
put(char)	Writes a character (like C's `putchar` and `fputc`).
putback(char)	Puts back a character (like C's `ungetc`).
read(char *, int)	Binary read (like C's `fread`).
write(const char *, int)	Binary write (like C's `fwrite`).

Unlike C's **fread** and **fwrite** functions, the first argument to both **read** and **write** has type `char *` not `void *`. As a result, when you are reading or writing anything other than characters, an explicit cast is needed in the call.

There are several member functions that perform the same task as some of the manipulators: `fill` is equivalent to `setfill`, `width` is equivalent to `setw`, and `precision` is equivalent to `setprecision`. For example, `cout.width(10)` is equivalent to `cout << setw(10)`.

C++ provides a number of member functions to assist with error detection and recovery. They are:

Error Processing Functions

Function	Purpose
bad	Indicates if an unrecoverable error occurred.
clear	Sets or clears the internal error state.
eof	Returns end-of-file status.
fail	Indicates if an unrecoverable error or expected condition occurred.
good	Indicates if there is an error condition.
rdstate	Returns the current error state.

Refer to your implementation's I/O streams documentation for more information on these member functions.

File I/O

To perform file I/O, we must use `fstream.h` instead of `iostream.h`. This new header defines three file I/O classes called `ifstream`, `ofstream`, and `fstream`, which are used for input, output, and input/output files, respectively. These streams are designed for disk file I/O.

The following simple example copies an existing file to a newly created file, converting each input character to lowercase:

```
#include <fstream.h>
#include <ctype.h>

main()
{
        ifstream infile;
        ofstream outfile;
        char c;

        infile.open("input.dat");
        if (infile.fail()) {
                cerr << "Can't open input file\n";
                return 1;
        }
```

```
        outfile.open("output.dat");
        if (outfile.fail()) {
                cerr << "Can't open output file\n";
                return 2;
        }

        while ((c = infile.get()) != EOF) {
                outfile.put(tolower(c));
        }

        infile.close();
        outfile.close();

        return 0;
}
```

`infile` and `outfile` are user-defined input and output stream objects, respectively. The underlying files are manipulated via the stream member functions `open`, `close`, `get`, and `put`. The state of the stream object can be checked at any time, as shown with the `fail` function, to see if the stream has encountered an error. The expression `infile.fail()` is equivalent to `!infile`, as the `!` operator has been defined to work with objects of these I/O classes.

The following example is a slight variation of the previous one, except that a function is called to do the file manipulation, and the filenames are passed in as arguments:

```
#include <fstream.h>
#include <ctype.h>

void filecopy(const char *ifilename, const char *ofilename);

main()
{
        filecopy("file1.dat", "file2.dat");

        return 0;
}
void filecopy(const char *ifilename, const char *ofilename)
{
        ifstream infile(ifilename);
        ofstream outfile(ofilename);
        char c;

        if (!infile) {
                cerr << "Can't open input file " << ifilename << "\n";
                return;
        }
```

```
            if (!outfile) {
                    cerr << "Can't open output file " << ofilename << "\n";
                    return;
            }
            while ((c = infile.get()) != EOF) {
                    outfile.put(tolower(c));
            }
}
```

While this example achieves the same result, there are no explicit calls to **open** and **close**. In the previous example, the two stream objects were created but not explicitly initialized. That is, the default constructor was invoked for each. In this example, we explicitly initialize the objects when they are defined, causing the files to actually be opened by the constructor. Similarly, the files are not explicitly closed, as that is handled by the stream destructors. You need to use **open** and **close** directly only if you want to recycle a stream object for different files.

The constructor, as well as the **open** member function, has an optional second argument that identifies the open mode to use. An enumerated type is defined with a set of enumeration constants, one for each mode. The set of enumeration constants is as follows:

File Open Mode Bits

Name	Purpose
app	Appends mode.
ate	Seeks to eof on open.
binary	Binary file.
in	Opens for read.
nocreate	Open fails if file does not exist.
noreplace	Open fails if file already exists.
out	Opens for write.
trunc	Truncates file if it already exists.

As each enumeration constant is a power of 2, you can OR them together. The enumeration constant names belong to the predefined class **ios**, so to refer to them we must qualify them with **ios::**. For example:

```
ofstream myfile("file.dat", ios::noreplace | ios::binary);
```

For input file streams, **ios::in** is always implied, whether you specify it or not. Similarly, for output file streams, **ios::out** is always implied. However, for a file of class **fstream** (one open for both input and output), no default mode is implied; one must always be supplied.

C's file model permits random positioning via the functions **ftell**, **fgetpos**, **fseek**, and **fsetpos**. C++ provides an equivalent set, as follows:

Input and Input/Output Random Access

Function	Purpose
`seekg(streampos)`	Seeks to absolute position.
`seekg(streamoff, ios::seek_dir)`	Seeks to relative position.
`streamoff tellg()`	Reports current position.

Output and Input/Output Random Access

Function	Purpose
`seekp(streampos)`	Seeks to absolute position.
`seekp(streamoff, ios::seek_dir)`	Seeks to relative position.
`streamoff tellp()`	Reports current position.

The relative offset base may be one of the enumeration constants **beg**, **cur**, or **end**. (These correspond to C's **SEEK_SET**, **SEEK_CUR**, and **SEEK_END**, respectively.) Because these are part of the class **ios**, they must be qualified with **ios::**, as we saw with the format state flags earlier.

You can also read from, and write to, files using the extraction and insertion operators. For example:

```
#include <fstream.h>
#include <iomanip.h>

main()
{
        ofstream outfile("test.dat");

        outfile << setfill('*') << setw(6) << 34 << '\n';

        return 0;
}
```

The resulting file test.dat contains the following data:

```
****34
```

String Encoding and Decoding

C permits encoding and decoding of strings using `sprintf` and `sscanf`, respectively. C++ provides the same capability via the header `strstream.h`, as follows:

String Encoding and Decoding

```cpp
        #include <strstream.h>
        #include <iomanip.h>
        #include <string.h>

        main()
        {
                char str[40], c;
                int i;
                double d;

/*1*/           ostrstream(str, sizeof(str)) << 123 << " abcdef "
                        << setw(8) << setprecision(2)
                        << setiosflags(ios::fixed) << 123.789 << ends;

                cout << '|' << str << "| strlen(str) = " << strlen(str) << '\n';

/*2*/           istrstream("123abcd4.56") >> i >> c >> setw(3) >> str >> c >> d;

                cout << "i = " << i << ", str =|" << str << "|, d = " << d << '\n';

                return 0;
        }
```

The output produced is:

```
|123 abcdef   123.79| strlen(str) = 19
i = 123, str =|bc|, d = 4.56
```

In case 1, the constructor `ostrstream` is called to create a temporary, unnamed stream object. It establishes the array `str` as an output string for encoding. The array's length must be provided so overflow checking can be done. Once the object has been constructed, we write to that stream just like any other output stream. A trailing null character is not automatically added, so we use `ends` to add one.

In case 2, the constructor `istrstream` is called to create a temporary, unnamed stream object. It establishes the string literal as an input string for decoding. The array's length need not be provided. Once the object has been constructed, we read from that stream just like any other input stream. We wish to skip over the characters 'a' and 'd'. However, no manipulator is provided for this. Instead, we read them into the same `char` variable, one after the other. The `setw(3)` manipulator indicates that two characters should be read into `str` and a trailing null should be appended.

We also can create named objects of these string stream types. We can use this approach to construct a string in a number of output statements. For example:

```
ostrstream os(str, sizeof(str));

os << 123 << " abcdef ";
os << setw(8) << setprecision(2);
os << setiosflags(ios::fixed) << 123.789 << ends;
```

You very likely will stumble on a shortcoming of the standard I/O library when using `istrstream`. The problem arises when you are decoding strings that have the `const` qualifier. Consider the following example:

```
#include <strstream.h>

int get_value(const char *str)
{
        int i;

        istrstream((char *)str) >> i;

        return i;
}
```

The AT&T library, which most vendors mimic, has no constructor for `istrstream` that takes a `const`-qualified string. Therefore, you must explicitly cast away the `const` property, as shown. Hopefully this problem will be fixed by Standard C++.

User-Defined Manipulators

We can easily write our own manipulators[2]. For example:

```
#include <iostream.h>

ostream &clearscreen(ostream &os);
ostream &blink(ostream &os);
ostream &reset(ostream &os);

main()
{
        cout << clearscreen << "Top of screen "
             << blink << "blinking too"
             << reset << "normal\n";

        return 0;
}
```

---

[2]The coverage provided here is only intended to show how to write simple manipulators. A more detailed coverage is outside the scope of this book.

User-Defined Manipulators

```
ostream &clearscreen(ostream &os)
{
        return os << "\33[2J";   // ANSI clear-screen sequence
}

ostream &blink(ostream &os)
{
        return os << "\33[5m";   // ANSI set blink sequence
}

ostream &reset(ostream &os)
{
        return os << "\33[0m";   // ANSI reset sequence
}
```

Manipulators with one argument of type `int` can be defined using the macro `OMANIP` defined in `iomanip.h`, as follows:

```
#include <iostream.h>
#include <iomanip.h>

ostream &sp(ostream &os, int count)
{
        for (int i = 0; i < count; ++i)
                os << ' ';

        return os;
}

OMANIP(int) space(int i)
{
        return OMANIP(int)(sp, i);
}

main()
{
        cout << "***" << space(3)
             << "***" << space(5)
             << "***\n";

        return 0;
}
```

The output produced is:

```
***   ***     ***
```

The same approach can be used for manipulators with one argument of type `long`. Manipulators with other argument types or with more than one argument can also be handled. These require the use of the macro `IOMANIPdeclare` and will not be discussed further here.

Part III

Writing Your Own Simple Classes

Chapter 7

Classes and Objects

Classes are one of the main concepts underlying the object-oriented extensions C++ makes to C. Simply stated, a *class* is a special kind of structure that uses the keyword `class` in place of `struct`.

In this chapter, we will learn about *encapsulation*. Encapsulation is the process whereby members of a structure can be hidden from general access and where access to those members and their associated functions can be controlled.

Introduction to Classes

A potential problem with structures is that any code that can access a structure object as a whole can also access all its members. C provides no way to limit access to members within a structure.

The problem, then, becomes one of a lack of discipline. If you can get at any member of a structure in scope, you do so, generally in a rather haphazard way. That is, the way in which you interface with such objects is not controlled, making debugging and maintenance more difficult. If you could limit the ways in which objects could be accessed, it would be much easier to debug cases in which these objects get inadvertently overwritten. It would also be easier to maintain the code, as you would need to look at only those functions having access in order to learn about the underlying object.

A class permits you to partition the members in an object of that class into two main groups[1]: private and public. You do this using the `public` *access specifier* keyword so that it looks like a C-style label, as shown in the class definition for `CircleB` in the following example:

```
struct CircleA {
        long xorigin;
        long yorigin;
        unsigned long radius;
};
```

---
[1] A third category, protected, is outside the scope of this book.

```
class CircleB {
public:
        long xorigin;
        long yorigin;
        unsigned long radius;
};
```

All members below the public boundary are public and can be accessed in the same way as structure members. However, as you might expect, most class members are made private, so access to them is restricted.

In the example above, and in almost all other examples following throughout the book, the class definition is placed at the beginning of the same source module containing the rest of the program. While this is permitted in C++, just as it is in C for structure and union definitions, it is good style to place class definitions in headers. (Of course, nontrivial programs will also have more than one source module.) Hiding things in headers is a valuable way of applying abstraction. However, as our `Circle` class will continually be modified and/or extended, and the reader must be shown these changes, hiding class details in a text such as this is not appropriate. As a result, class definitions are not hidden, except in the solutions to the lab exercises.

Data Privacy

In the following example, two class members are private while one is public:

```
class Circle {
        long xorigin;
public:
        unsigned long radius;
private:
        long yorigin;
};

main()
{
        Circle c;
        void f(Circle *p);

        c.xorigin = 5;          // error, member is private
        c.radius = 6;

        f(&c);

        return 0;
}
```

```
void f(Circle *p)
{
        p->xorigin = 5;         // error, member is private
        p->radius = 6;
}
```

In `main`, even though object `c` is in scope, we cannot access the private member `xorigin` directly. And when we pass the address of `c` to function `f`, we are likewise prohibited from accessing that member. On the other hand, the public member `radius` is directly and indirectly accessible by name, as shown.

C++ programmers often say that `c` is an *instance* of the object type `Circle` or that `c` is an *instantiation* of that type.

By default, all members of a class are private; it is as if there is an occurrence of the `private` access specifier keyword before the first member is declared. We can explicitly use the `private` keyword. In this case, we have one implicitly private member, one explicitly public member, and one explicitly private member. The simple approach is to declare all the private members first, followed by the `public` keyword and then the public members.

To access the private members, we need to learn about member functions.

Member Functions

C permits two levels of function linkage: internal and external. These are achieved via the `static` and `extern` keywords, respectively. A `static` function is callable from anywhere inside the source file in which it is defined, while an `extern` function is globally callable. C++ provides a much finer granularity of access to functions, as we will see in the next few sections. The designer of a class can limit member access to a specified set of functions:

```
#include <iostream.h>

class Circle {
        long xorigin;
        long yorigin;
        unsigned long radius;
public:
        void init(long xo, long yo, unsigned long rad);
        void print(const char *name);
};
```

In this case, all the data members are private. However, there are two function prototypes in the public section. This may look rather unusual, because it appears that an object of that class contains those functions. This is not the case, however. These functions, called *member functions*, are the only functions that are authorized to directly access the private members.

Now that we have established that the private members can be accessed only from the functions `init` and `print`, how do we call those functions? The following example shows how:

```
main()
{
        Circle c1;
        Circle c2;

        c1.init(5, 4, 10);
        c1.print("c1");

        c2.init(2, 9, 5);
        c2.print("c2");

        return 0;
}
```

The key lies in the expression `c1.init(5, 4, 10)`. This is a call to the member function init. It may look strange to C programmers to call a function using such notation, but given the way in which the class is defined, it makes perfect sense. To reference a member, we use the dot operator, and if that member is a function, we then call it using the ( ) function call operator. You cannot call that member function unless you are operating on an object of that class. Specifically, `c1.init(...)` calls the init function to operate directly on the object c1. And as you might expect, `c2.init(...)` invokes init to operate on object c2.

Of course, `c1.print(...)` and `c2.print(...)` call print to operate on the objects c1 and c2, respectively.

How then are these member functions defined? The syntax must be somehow different, because presumably, we can also have a regular function of the same name. In fact, we could even have two member functions with the same name, each for a different class. The solution is to qualify the function name with its class name. That is, `Circle::init` and `Circle::print` declare that these two functions are member functions for the class Circle. For example:

```
void Circle::init(long xo, long yo, unsigned long rad)
{
        xorigin = xo;
        yorigin = yo;
        radius = rad;
}

void Circle::print(const char *name)
{
        cout << "Circle " << name << " := (" << xorigin << ':'
             << yorigin << ':' << radius   << ")\n";
}
```

These functions both contain a surprise. Nowhere do we qualify to which object we are referring; we simply use the member names within that class without preceding them with a dot or arrow operator. This is impossible in C, except with the `offsetof` macro in `stddef.h`. In all

Member Functions

other contexts, a member name must be explicitly qualified with a structure or union designator or a pointer to such an object type. The reason no qualification is needed in C++ is that when the functions are called, the calls are implicitly qualified by the object being operated on. That is, when these functions execute, they intuitively know which object on which to operate. (We will talk more of how this is implemented and how to access the "current object" using the **this** keyword in chapter 8, "Member Functions Revisited.")

The output produced is:

```
Circle c1 := (5:4:10)
Circle c2 := (2:9:5)
```

Let's take this one step further and look at an example in which not only is the same name used for member functions in different classes, but it is also a nonmember function name as well:

```
#include <iostream.h>

class Circle {
        long xorigin;
        long yorigin;
        unsigned long radius;
public:
        void init(long xo, long yo, unsigned long rad);
        void print(const char *name);
};

class Rectangle {
        long xorigin;
        long yorigin;
        unsigned long xlen;
        unsigned long ylen;
public:
        void init(long xo, long yo, unsigned long xl, unsigned long yl);
        void print(const char *name);
};

void print(const char *text);    // non-member function

main()
{
        Circle c;
        Rectangle r;

        c.init(0, 0, 0);
        r.init(0, 0, 0, 0);
```

```
        c.print("c");
        r.print("r");
        print("Text");

        return 0;
}
```

We now have three functions called **print**: one member function each for classes **Circle** and **Rectangle**, and one nonmember function.

If you call function **print** from inside member function **init** for an object of class **Circle**, you actually will be calling **Circle::print**. That is, the same name used in an outer scope will be hidden. If, however, you wish to call the nonclass function **print** instead, you have to use the scope resolution operator ::, as follows:

```
void Circle::init(long xo, long yo, unsigned long rad)
{
        xorigin = xo;
        yorigin = yo;
        radius = rad;
        print("Circle");        // call Circle::print
        ::print("Circle");      // call generic print
}
```

Thus far, we have seen that any function having access to an object of a given class has immediate access to the public member functions of that class.

You can make member functions private by declaring them inside the private section of the class, as follows:

```
#include <iostream.h>

class Circle {
        // ...
        void secret();          // private member function
public:
        // ...
};

main()
{
        Circle c;

        c.secret();             // error, secret is private

        return 0;
}
```

Now we can no longer access the member function using the notation established earlier; the function has been hidden. How then can we access this function? A private member function can be called only by another public or private member function of the same class, as follows:

```cpp
#include <iostream.h>

class Circle {
        // ...
        void secret();   // private member function
public:
        void init(long xo, long yo, unsigned long rad);
        // ...
};

main()
{
        Circle c;

        c.init(5, 4, 10);

        return 0;
}

void Circle::init(long xo, long yo, unsigned long rad)
{
        xorigin = xo;
        yorigin = yo;
        radius = rad;
        secret();
}

void Circle::secret()
{
        cout << "Inside function secret\n";
}
```

The output produced is:

```
Inside function secret
```

Here, the user calls the public member function **init**, which in turn calls the private member function **secret**. In this manner, the designer of the class can rigidly define the interface between the program and class members. You can argue that a well-disciplined programmer can achieve the same result simply by not doing silly or unreasonable things. The problem here is that it is left to the programmer to make sure no rules are broken, whereas in C++ all this privacy and associated protection is forced on you once the class is designed. On a nontrivial project, you should find the cost of forcing this discipline is far outweighed by the benefits of reduced debugging and maintenance.

A word of caution to the C folks. C lends itself to abuse, and many C programmers have quite a cavalier approach to writing programs in that language. That will not work with C++ if you intend to exploit it properly. If your C code is rather undisciplined and you intend to write C++ that way, there's not much point in changing languages. If you insist on putting all your members in the public section of a class, you may as well use C instead.

Restricted Global Data

Most languages support the notion of global variables—ones that can be accessed from anywhere in the program. C provides this capability and also allows a restricted global scope via file-scope `statics`. C then has three levels of visibility for data: block, source file, and program.

C++ supports the same levels of privacy. It also allows the concepts of a global object and a class to be combined by allowing data members of a class to be shared by multiple objects of that class type, via the keyword `static`, as shown below. `static` is the only storage class keyword permitted in data declarations in a class. The following example shows how `static` is used in this context:

```
#include <iostream.h>

class Circle {
        long xorigin;
        long yorigin;
        static unsigned long count;     // static member
        unsigned long radius;
public:
        void set_count(unsigned long c);
        void init(long xo, long yo, unsigned long rad);
        void print(const char *name);
};

unsigned long Circle::count;    // static member definition

main()
{
        Circle c1;
        Circle c2;
        Circle c3;

        c1.init(0, 0, 0);
        c2.init(0, 0, 0);
        c3.init(0, 0, 0);
```

```
                c1.set_count(10);      // set one count

                c1.print("c1");        // look at all counts
                c2.print("c2");
                c3.print("c3");

                cout << "\nsizeof(c1) = " << sizeof(c1) << '\n';
                cout << "Sum of sizes of the four individual members = "
                     << sizeof(long) * 4 << '\n';

                return 0;
        }
        void Circle::set_count(unsigned long c)
        {
                count = c;
        }
        void Circle::print(const char *name)
        {
                cout << "Circle " << (name == 0 ? "??" : name) << " := ("
                     << xorigin << ':' << yorigin << ':' << radius << ")\t";
                     << "count = " << count    << '\n';
        }
```

The output produced from one implementation is:

```
        Circle c1 := (0:0:0)     count = 10
        Circle c2 := (0:0:0)     count = 10
        Circle c3 := (0:0:0)     count = 10

        sizeof(c1) = 12
        Sum of sizes of the four individual members = 16
```

The **static** member **count** is declared like, behaves like, and is accessed like a non-**static** member. However, it is not actually stored as part of any class object. As evidenced by the output, the size of each of c1, c2, and c3 is 12 bytes, the sum of the sizes of the three non-**static** members. **count** is allocated space but it is not physically part of any of the class objects.

When you declare a **static** member, you must also provide a separate definition for the actual object *without* using the keyword **static**, as shown above in:

```
        unsigned long Circle::count;    // static member definition
```

When we set **count** to be 10 for object c1, the **count** for c2 and c3 also "became" 10. **count**, then, is like a global object but one that can be accessed only by member functions of the class to which it belongs.

In the following example, no space ever is allocated for an object of class `Circle`. However, space always is allocated for `static` members, even if no objects of that class exist:

```
#include <iostream.h>

class Circle {
        long xorigin;
        long yorigin;
        unsigned long radius;
public:
        static unsigned long count;     // static member
};

unsigned long Circle::count;    // static member definition

main()
{
        cout << "count = "             << Circle::count << '\n';
        cout << "sizeof(count) = "     << sizeof(Circle::count) << '\n';
        cout << "&count = "            << &Circle::count << '\n';

        return 0;
}
```

You can declare a `static` member in the public section of a class. As a result, that member can be accessed from outside a member function. To do so, you must qualify the member name by the class name and the scope resolution operator ::, as shown.

`static` Member Functions

We also can make member functions `static`, as follows:

```
#include <iostream.h>

class Circle {
        long xorigin;
        long yorigin;
        static unsigned long count;     // static member
        unsigned long radius;
        static void test1();
public:
        static void test2();
};

unsigned long Circle::count;    // static member definition
```

```
main()
{
        Circle c1;

        c1.test2();
        Circle::test2();

        return 0;
}
void Circle::test1()
{
        count = 1;
        xorigin = 0;     // error, not static
}
void Circle::test2()
{
        count = 1;
        xorigin = 0;     // error, not static
        test1();
}
```

`static` functions are permitted to access only `static` data members. And as `static` data member objects are created separate from objects of the class, you do not even need a class object to call a `static` function. For example, we simply used the call `Circle::test2()`. This makes more sense than does `c1.test2()`, because the object name used here is irrelevant—the `static` data members belong to all objects of that class.

const- and volatile-Qualified Member Functions

The type qualifiers `const` and `volatile` are defined for functions as well as data. When they are used with functions, the qualification applies to the object being operated on. For example:

```
class Circle {
        long xorigin;
        long yorigin;
        unsigned long radius;
        static unsigned long count;
public:
        void f1();
        void f2() const;
        void f3() volatile;
        void f4() const volatile;
};
```

```
unsigned long Circle::count;

main()
{
        Circle c1;
        const Circle c2 = c1;
        volatile Circle c3;
        const volatile Circle c4 = c1;

        c1.f1();
        c1.f2();
        c1.f3();
        c1.f4();

        c2.f1();           // error, c2 is const but f1 is not
        c2.f2();
        c2.f3();           // error, c2 is const but f3 is not
        c2.f4();

        c3.f1();           // error, c3 is volatile but f1 is not
        c3.f2();           // error, c3 is volatile but f2 is not
        c3.f3();
        c3.f4();

        c4.f1();           // error, c4 is const/volatile but f1 is not
        c4.f2();           // error, c4 is const/volatile but f2 is not
        c4.f3();           // error, c4 is const/volatile but f3 is not
        c4.f4();

        return 0;
}
```

If an object is const- or volatile-qualified, it can be used only with calls to member functions that are like-qualified. In the absence of a const qualifier on a member function, the compiler assumes that function will modify the object on which it is operating. Similarly, if the function is not volatile-qualified, there is no point in passing in the address of a volatile object, as the function will not respect its volatility. *As a result, you should make every member function you possibly can be const-qualified so you can call it for const objects as well as non-const objects.* As the volatile qualifier is much more specialized, and probably less likely to be used, you need to use it with functions only when you are absolutely sure volatile objects are likely to exist.

Here are the member functions:

```
void Circle::f1()
{
        radius = 0;     // OK
        count = 0;      // OK
}

void Circle::f2() const
{
        radius = 0;     // error, attempt to modify const
        count = 0;      // OK
}

void Circle::f3() volatile
{
        radius = 0;     // OK
        count = 0;      // OK
}

void Circle::f4() const volatile
{
        radius = 0;     // error, attempt to modify const
        count = 0;      // OK
}
```

If you are designing a general-purpose class and do not know whether `volatile` objects will ever be used, you need to make a decision as to whether you will always or never support them. One solution is as follows:

```
#ifdef NO_VOLATILE
#define volatile        // cause 'volatile' to be removed
#endif

void Circle::f4() const volatile
{
        // ...
}
```

By putting `volatile` in all of the right places, you can conditionally define a macro by that name to expand either to nothing or to the keyword `volatile`. In this manner, the class easily can be made to support `volatile` objects.

Note that a `const` function can modify non-`const` `static` members even though it cannot modify non-`static` members. Because `static` members are not actually stored in the class object, they are not covered by that object's `const` qualification.

A `const` member function never can call a non-`const` member function. Similarly, a `volatile` member function never can call a non-`volatile` member function. For example:

```
#include <iostream.h>

class Circle {
        long xorigin;
        long yorigin;
        unsigned long radius;
public:
        void fun1() const;
        void fun2();
};

main()
{
        Circle c1;

        c1.fun1();

        return 0;
}

void Circle::fun1() const
{
        cout << "In fun1" << '\n';
        fun2();         // error, fun2 is non-const
}

void Circle::fun2()
{
        cout << "In fun2" << '\n';
}
```

Enumerated Types and typedefs

A class definition may contain things other than data and function members. In particular, it may contain definitions of enumerated types and type synonyms created via **typedef**, as follows:

```
class Circle {
        enum color1 {black, white};             // private
        typedef int count1;                     // private
public:
        enum color2 {red, green, blue};         // public
        typedef int count2;                     // public
        void test();
};
```

```cpp
#include <iostream.h>

main()
{
        Circle c;
/*1*/   Circle::color1 col1 = Circle::black;    // 2 errors
/*2*/   Circle::color2 col2 = Circle::blue;     // OK
/*3*/   Circle::count1 x1 = 10;                 // 1 error
/*4*/   Circle::count2 x2 = 20;                 // OK

        c.test();

        return 0;
}

void Circle::test()
{
/*5*/   color1 col1 = black;    // OK
/*6*/   color2 col2 = red;      // OK
/*7*/   count1 x1 = 10;         // OK
/*8*/   count2 x2 = 20;         // OK
}
```

The enumerated types `color1` and `color2` and all their enumeration constant names, and the type synonyms `count1` and `count2`, are *specific* to class `Circle`. As such, their use is subject to the scoping rules of classes. In particular, the public names `color2` (and its enumeration constants) and `count2` are accessible to the outside world only via the scope resolution operator `::`, as shown. However, the private names `color1` (and its enumeration constants) and `count1` are not available to the outside world.

While a `static` member function has no access to non-`static` data and function members, it can access all enumerated type names, enumeration constants, and type synonyms defined for its class.

Classes, Structures, and Unions

In C++, the term *class* includes types defined using any of the keywords `class`, `struct`, and `union`. Unless otherwise stated, objects of these types have the same general properties and capabilities. For example, all three types may have public and private members. However, because of their nature, unions are more restricted than class and structure types. For example, a union may not contain a `static` data member. Also, an anonymous union cannot have members that are `private`, nor can it have member functions.

All class types may contain bit-fields. While C requires that a bit-field have one of the types `int`, `signed int`, or `unsigned int`, C++ permits them to have any integral type. In C++, enumerated types are not considered to be integral types, so bit-fields of such types are not permitted even though they are common extensions in C compilers.

If a class is defined inside a function definition, it is called a *local class*. The class name is local to its enclosing scope. A local class cannot have `static` data members, and if it has member functions, they must be defined inline.

Nested Classes

Like C, C++ permits structure and union definitions to be nested. That is, a structure or union definition can occur inside another structure or union definition. Of course, C++ extends this to classes as well. However, in C the tags and member names of nested classes are public, whereas in C++ they are private to their *enclosing class*. Consider the following example:

```
class L1 {
        typedef int L1count;
        enum L1color {red, blue};
        int L1i;
        static int L1si;
public:
        struct L2A {
                typedef int L2Acount;
                enum L2Acolor {green, white};
                static int L2Asi;
                void L2Af();

        private:
                int L2Ai;
        } s;

        union L2B {
                typedef int L2Bcount;
                enum L2Bcolor {yellow, brown};
                int L2Bi;
                double L2Bd;
                void L2Bf();
        } u;
        void L1f();
};

int L1::L1si = 0;
int L1::L2A::L2Asi = 0;
```

Class L1 contains a type synonym, an enumerated type, four data members, and one member function. Two of its data members (s and u) are class objects whose class types are also defined at the point of the object declaration. L2A and L2B are nested classes within L1, and L1 is an enclosing class of L2A and L2B. And while L2A and L2B have a common enclosing scope, each of these has its own scope separate from the other.

The classes L2A and L2B are defined much as L1 is, except that L2B has no **static** data member. All identifier names reflect their level in the nested hierarchy: L1 denotes level 1, L2A denotes level 2 class A, and L2B denotes level 2 class B.

The **private** access specifier applies to L2A only and not to L1.

Let's try to access some of the class members from a nonmember function:

```
void f()
{
        L1 x1;

        x1.L1i = 20;            // error, private member
        x1.s.L2Asi = 20;
        x1.s.L2Ai = 20;         // error, private member
        x1.u.L2Bi = 20;

        L2A x2a;                // error, different scope
        L2B x2b;                // error, different scope
}
```

The nonmember function f can access only public members of L1. And as the tags L2A and L2B are local to L1, they are not accessible outside that class. We could, however, use L2A and L2B by specifying their full names—L1::L2A and L1::L2B, respectively.

The following function is a member of the nested class L2A:

```
void L1::L2A::L2Af()
{
        L1count count1;
        L2Acount count2;
        L2Bcount count3;        // error, different scope
        L1color color1 = red;
        L2Acolor color2 = green;
        L2Bcolor color3 = brown;// error, different scope
        L1i = 10;               // error, non-static member
        L2Ai = 10;
        L2Bi = 10;              // error, different scope
        L1si = 20;
        L2Asi = 20;
}
```

As L2Af is a member function in a nested class, its name must be qualified by all its ancestors' names, as shown. This function can access all type synonyms, enumerated types, and **static** members from its enclosing class. However, it cannot access anything in its sister class L2B.

Here is the source for the member function L2Bf:

```
void L1::L2B::L2Bf()
{
        L1count count1;
        L2Acount count2;        // error, different scope
        L2Bcount count3;
        L1color color1 = red;
        L2Acolor color2 = green;// error, different scope
        L2Bcolor color3 = brown;
        L1i = 10;               // error, non-static member
        L2Ai = 10;              // error, different scope
        L2Bi = 10;
        L1si = 20;
        L2Asi = 20;             // error, different scope
}
```

Like `L2Af`, `L2Bf` is also a member function in a nested class. And while it can access most things in its enclosing class, it cannot access anything in its sister class `L2A`.

Here is the source for the function `L1f`:

```
void L1::L1f()
{
        L1count count1;
        L2Acount count2;        // error, subordinate scope
        L2Bcount count3;        // error, subordinate scope
        L1color color1 = red;
        L2Acolor color2 = green;// error, subordinate scope
        L2Bcolor color3 = brown;// error, subordinate scope
        L1i = 10;
        L2Ai = 10;              // error, subordinate scope
        L2Bi = 10;              // error, subordinate scope
        L1si = 20;
        L2Asi = 20;             // error, subordinate scope
}
```

`L1f` is a member function in an enclosing class. As such, it cannot access anything in the classes nested below it.

We saw that you must use multiple class names when defining member functions for nested classes. The notation used can be abbreviated by creating a type synonym for a nested class name path, as follows:

```
typedef L1::L2A GroupA;
typedef L1::L2B GroupB;

int L1::L1si = 0;
int GroupA::L2Asi = 0;
```

```
void GroupA::L2Af() { /* ... */ }

void GroupB::L2Bf() { /* ... */ }
```

Relaxing Class Member Access Restrictions

Until now, access to private members of a class has been restricted to member functions of that class. However, sometimes it is useful to give functions from outside that class the same access. You do this by making them *friend functions*, as follows:

```
class Rectangle;                    // tentative definition

class Circle {
        long xorigin;
        long yorigin;
        // ...
public:
        friend void share1(Circle *pc, Rectangle *pr);
        void share2(Rectangle *pr);
};
```

We have two classes that refer to each other. Class `Rectangle` is tentatively defined so that it can be referenced before its actual definition is seen. Function `share1` is a nonmember function that has been given permission to access the private members of `Circle`.

Here is the definition of the class `Rectangle`:

```
class Rectangle {
        long xorigin;
        long yorigin;
        // ...
public:
        friend void share1(Circle *pc, Rectangle *pr);
        friend void Circle::share2(Rectangle *pr);
};
```

The nonmember function `share1` has also been given permission to access the private members of `Rectangle`, as has the member function `share2` from class `Circle`:

```
void share1(Circle *pc, Rectangle *pr)   // friend to Circle and Rectangle
{
        pc->xorigin = 5;
        pr->xorigin = 6;
}
```

```
void Circle::share2(Rectangle *pr)        // friend to Rectangle
{
        pr->xorigin = 6;
}
```

In cases in which multiple member functions in one class need to access private members of another class, the whole second class can be made a friend of the first, as follows:

```
class Circle {
        friend class Rectangle;
        // ...
};
```

Pointers to Class Members

In C and C++, we have both pointers to objects and pointers to functions. In C, a pointer to an object can point to objects of a given type, regardless of where they are located. Whether they are part of a structure or union is of no consequence, because all members of a structure or union are accessible if the parent structure or union is accessible. If member functions were allowed to assign the address of a private member to a global pointer, we could access that private member via that pointer, thus bypassing the usual class-access restrictions.

With the extra access checking in C++, *pointers to members* are treated differently than are pointers to nonmember objects and functions. Specifically, a pointer to member is not assignment-compatible to a pointer to an object or function. Furthermore, a pointer to member is not even assignment-compatible to a pointer to void. However, it is assignment-compatible to the integer constant expression having value zero.

A pointer to member may be converted explicitly into a different pointer to member type if both types are pointers to members of the same class. From this statement, we can deduce that pointers to members are tied to a specific class by some syntactic means. The following example shows how:

```
#include <iostream.h>

class Test {
public:
        int pubi;
};

main()
{
        Test t = {20};
        Test *pt = &t;
/*1*/   int Test::*ctpi;

/*2*/   ctpi = &Test::pubi;
```

```
/*3*/      cout << "     t.*ctpi = " << t.*ctpi << '\n';
/*4*/      cout << "pt->*ctpi = " << pt->*ctpi << '\n';

           return 0;
}
```

The output produced is:

```
    t.*ctpi = 20
pt->*ctpi = 20
```

In case 1, ctpi is defined as a "pointer to int member of class Test." That is, a member pointer can only point to objects of a given type in a given class. And as was stated above, ctpi is not compatible and cannot be made compatible with a pointer to int. In case 2, this member pointer is assigned the "address" of the member pubi of the class Test. However, if you look closely at this assignment, you will notice that no object is actually referenced. Therein lies the difference between pointers to members and pointers to objects. The pointer to member ctpi has really been given the value of the offset[2] of the member pubi within the class Test.

Once a pointer to member is initialized, it is not actually associated with an object of the given class until it is used with one of two special operators, .* and ->*. In fact, the pointer to member is never permanently associated with any object. The expression t.*ctpi associates the pointer to the member pubi in the object t and dereferences the pointer, producing an int result. Similarly, the expression pt->*ctpi associates the pointer to the member pubi in the object pointed to by pt and dereferences the pointer, producing the same int result.

The pointer to member operators .* and ->* have their own level in the operator precedence table, immediately above the multiplicative operators *, /, and %. They associate left to right. These new operators are conceptually related to the member selection operators . and ->, which is the reason for the similarity in spelling.

The .* operator binds its right operand to its left operand, and the result is an object or function of the type specified by the right operand. The ->* operator also binds its right operand to its left operand, and the result is an object or function of the type specified by the right operand. The only difference between the two is that the left operand of .* must have a class type, while that of ->* must have a pointer to a class type. If a .* or ->* expression designates a function, the only operation that can be performed on that expression is to use it with the function call operator (). If the right operand of a .* or ->* expression is an lvalue, the whole expression is an lvalue.

Let's take a look at a larger example that involves pointers to member objects and functions as well as pointers to nonmember objects and functions. It highlights some (not necessarily obvious) pointer compatibility issues:

---

[2] A pointer to member might actually be implemented as a structure. Thus, the value of a pointer to member is not necessarily the address of some memory location.

```
#include <iostream.h>

class Test {
        int privi;
        static int privsi;
        void privf();
        static void privsf();
public:
        int pubi;
        static int pubsi;
        void pubf();
        static void pubsf();
};

int Test::privsi;
int Test::pubsi;
```

The class has two private objects and two private functions, one of each of which is also static. It also has two public objects and two public functions, one of each of which is also static. Much of the following example shows which members can be accessed and how:

```
main()
{
        Test t;
        Test *pt = &t;
        int i;
        int *pi;

/*1*/   pi = &i;
        pi = &t.pubi;
        pi = &t.pubsi;
        pi = &Test::pubsi;
```

Because the members pubi and pubsi are public, we can access both directly, and taking their address produces a pointer to int. We can also take the address of the public static data member pubsi without naming an object, since all objects of a class share the same copy of a static member. The important issue here is that we have taken the address of several members but have not produced a pointer to member type. Rather, we have produced expressions of type "pointer to object."

```
/*2*/   int Test::*ctpi;

/*3*/   ctpi = &Test::pubi;
        i = t.*ctpi;
        i = pt->*ctpi;
```

Pointers to Class Members

```
/*4*/    ctpi = &Test::pubsi;    // error
         ctpi = &i;              // error
         ctpi = pi;              // error
         pi = ctpi;              // error
```

In case 2, we have declared a pointer to member of type `int` in class `Test`. In case 3, this pointer is set to the member `pubi`, and we then use that pointer to member to access `pubi` in object `t` directly via the name `t` and indirectly via the pointer `pt`.

All four assignments in case 4 are invalid. The first is rejected simply because taking the address of a `static` data member produces a pointer to an object type, not a pointer to member type. The other three are rejected because pointers to objects and pointers to members are incompatible.

The source continues:

```
         void f();
         void (*pf)();

/*5*/    pf = &f;
         (*pf)();

/*6*/    pf = &t.pubf;           // error

/*7*/    pf = &t.pubsf;
         (*pf)();

/*8*/    pf = &Test::pubsf;
         (*pf)();
```

The notation for using pointers to public functions is just like that for using pointers to public objects, with one exception: We cannot take the address of a non-`static` member function by using the traditional notation. Member functions are different in this regard, because they really are not the same as a data member that happens to be a pointer to a function. We can, however, take the address of a `static` member function and call the underlying function.

In case 9, `ctpf` is defined to be a pointer to a member function, having the argument list and return type as shown, for class `Test`:

```
/*9*/    void (Test::*ctpf)();

/*10*/   ctpf = &Test::pubf;
         (t.*ctpf)();
         (pt->*ctpf)();
```

And in case 10, this pointer is associated with a specific member function. Then, in case 10, it is further associated with a particular class object.

The five assignments in case 11 are all rejected:

```
/*11*/  ctpf = &f;                  // error
        ctpf = &t.pubsf;            // error
        ctpf = &Test::pubsf;        // error
        ctpf = pf;                  // error
        pf = ctpf;                  // error

        return 0;
}
```

The first, fourth, and fifth are rejected because pointers to member functions are not compatible with pointers to functions; and the second and third because pointers to members cannot point at **static** members of a class.

The source continues:

```
void f()
{
        cout << "Inside regular function f\n";
}

void Test::privf()
{
        cout << "Inside private member function privf\n";

        int *pi;
        int Test::*ctpi;

/*12*/  pi = &privi;
        ctpi = &privi;              // error
```

Within the private member function `privf`, the addresses of private non-**static** member objects are used with the usual pointer-to-object notation. In fact, we cannot use pointer-to-member notation. `privf` continues:

```
        void (*pf)();
        void (Test::*ctpf)();

/*13*/  pf = &privf;                // error
        pf = &Test::privf;          // error
        pf = &privsf;
/*14*/  pf = &Test::pubf;           // error
        pf = &pubsf;
```

```
                ctpf = &Test::privf;
/*15*/  ctpf = &privsf;            // error
                ctpf = &Test::pubf;
/*16*/  ctpf = &pubsf;             // error
}
```

Pointers to functions can point only to `static` member functions, and pointers to member functions can point only to non-`static` member functions.

The remaining functions follow:

```
void Test::privsf()
{
        cout << "Inside private static member function privsf\n";
}

void Test::pubf()
{
        cout << "Inside public member function pubf\n";
}

void Test::pubsf()
{
        cout << "Inside public static member function pubsf\n";
}
```

When all the erroneous lines in the program above are removed, the resulting program produces the following output:

```
Inside regular function f
Inside public static member function pubsf
Inside public static member function pubsf
Inside public member function pubf
Inside public member function pubf
```

As defined in `iostream.h`, the I/O operators `<<` and `>>` cannot handle operands of type "pointer to member," and since expressions of this type cannot be converted to `void *`, there is no standard way to read or write such values.

Exercise 1

Define a class called Date that has three private integer members: day, month, and year. Dates for other than the 20th century must be supported. Define a member function called init that can be used to initialize a Date object. init is passed three arguments: year, month, and day, in that order. (If a year is less than 100, assume it is a year in the 20th century.)

Also define a member function called print that can be used to display the current contents of a Date object. The display format is dd-Mmm-yyyy, where dd has a leading zero for days less than 10. Months are displayed as Mmm, such that January is Jan, February is Feb, and so on.

Define and initialize some Date objects, and display their values. It would seem reasonable to check that the date being given to init is indeed valid. Implement the validation code by using conditional compilation directives so it can easily be disabled. Check the validation code by using a date of year −5, month 2.5, and day 260. (A leap year is one that either is a multiple of 4 but not a century, or is a multiple of 400.)

There are a number of integer types that can be used to represent the year, month, and day members. Implement your solution so that if one or more of these types is changed, the impact on the source is minimized.

Chapter 8

Member Functions Revisited

In this chapter, we will see how a member function "knows" about the object on which it is operating. We will also discuss using default arguments with member functions, and overloading and inlining of member functions.

Passing Objects to Member Functions

Member functions were introduced in chapter 7, "Classes and Objects," by the following example:

```
class Circle {
        long xorigin;
        long yorigin;
        unsigned long radius;
public:
        void init(long xo, long yo, unsigned long rad);
};

void Circle::init(long xo, long yo, unsigned long rad)
{
        xorigin = xo;
        yorigin = yo;
        radius = rad;
}
```

Inside the member function `init`, we can directly access the class members by name. This is possible because the member function "knows" on which object it is currently operating, so there is no need to use a member selection operator explicitly. How does it know this? When a member function is called, you specify the object on which it is to operate by the way in which the function is called. For example:

```
c1.init(5, 4, 10);
c2.init(2, 9, 5);
```

Here, `init` is called to operate on object `c1` and then on `c2`. Instead of requiring you to pass in the address of these objects directly, the compiler does this automatically. That is, whenever you call a non-`static` member function, a pointer to the object for which the member function is invoked is passed as a hidden argument. `static` member functions can access only `static` members, so they do not require and do not have a hidden argument. Similarly, nonmember functions have no hidden argument either.

The Hidden Argument

Inside the called member function, the hidden argument is available by name, even though it never is declared explicitly. The hidden, formal argument containing the object's address is called `this`. `this` is a C++ keyword that denotes a local variable of storage class `auto` that exists in every non-`static` member function. Its type is "pointer to object for which this member function was invoked." `this` can be used explicitly as follows:

```
void Circle::init(long xo, long yo, unsigned long rad)
{
        this->xorigin = xo;
        this->yorigin = yo;
        this->radius = rad;
}
```

In this example, all of the uses of `this->` can be omitted, and usually are, since they are redundant.

The variable `this` is defined and initialized before any local, automatic variables declared in your function, so it is available for use immediately when that function is entered.

Local/Member Name Conflicts

One possible time to use `this` in a member function is when you have local identifiers declared in that function that have the same names as members of the class. For example:

```
main()
{
        Circle c1;

        c1.init(5, 4, 10);
        c1.print("c1");

        return 0;
}
```

Passing Objects to Member Functions

```
void Circle::init(long xo, long yo, unsigned long rad)
{
        int xorigin;

        xorigin = xo;    // assigned to local variable
        yorigin = yo;
        radius = rad;
}
```

The output produced is:

```
Circle c1 := (???:4:10)
```

The `xorigin` that gets initialized is the local automatic variable by that name, not the `xorigin` member in the class object. This is shown by the fact that the class member `xorigin` was not explicitly initialized, and since c1 was automatic, its initial value is undefined (as indicated by "???"). To correct this, you must qualify `xorigin` specifically to indicate you wish to access the member instead, as follows:

```
        void Circle::init(long xo, long yo, unsigned long rad)
        {
                int xorigin;

                xorigin = xo;             /* local int */
/*1*/           this->xorigin = xo;       /* Circle object */
/*2*/           Circle::xorigin = xo;     /* Circle object */
                yorigin = yo;
                radius = rad;
        }
```

Cases 1 and 2 are equivalent; both access the member `xorigin`.

this and That

We have not yet seen any compelling need to access `this` by name. However, there are some cases in which it is needed. For example, a member function may be building a linked data structure, in which case it can use `this` when it needs to refer to the address of the current object it is adding to the list.

The name `this` also is needed in member functions that return their hidden argument by value, address, or reference. For example:

```
Circle Circle::larger(Circle c)
{
        return (radius > c.radius ? *this : c);
}
```

Member function `larger` returns by value the Circle that has the larger radius. If the hidden argument points to the larger object, that object must be returned by value by dereferencing `this`.

Although `this` is a local variable, you cannot modify it. The type of `this` ordinarily is:

class-type * const this

However, if the member function is `const`-qualified, the type is:

const *class-type* * const this

In `volatile`-qualified member functions, the type is:

volatile *class-type* * const this

And, of course, if a function is both `const`- and `volatile`-qualified, the type is:

const volatile *class-type* * const this

Overloading Member Functions

In chapter 7, "Classes and Objects," we saw that the same function name could be used in different classes. We now have several member functions with the same name in the same class. For example:

```
#include <iostream.h>

class Circle {
        long xorigin;
        long yorigin;
        unsigned long radius;
public:
        void init(long xo, long yo, unsigned long rad);
        void init(long xo, long yo);
        void init(unsigned long rad);
};
```

There are three member functions having the name `init`. All have the same return type, but their argument lists are different. Either they take a different number of arguments or the argument types are different. That is, their signatures are different.

Here is the main program:

```
main()
{
        Circle c;

        c.init(5, 4, 10);
        c.init(5, 4);
        c.init(10);

        return 0;
}
```

The three functions are disambiguated by the way in which they are called. For example, the expression c.init(5, 4, 10) invokes the version taking three arguments. The expression c.init(5, 4) invokes the version with two arguments, and c.init(10) invokes the version having one argument. The usual arithmetic promotion rules are applied so that char and short are promoted to int, just as in C.

Here are the definitions of the three initialization functions:

```
void Circle::init(long xo, long yo, unsigned long rad)
{
        cout << "init: 3 args\n";
        xorigin = xo;
        yorigin = yo;
        radius = rad;
}

void Circle::init(long xo, long yo)
{
        cout << "init: 2 args\n";
        xorigin = xo;
        yorigin = yo;
        radius = 1;     // default value
}

void Circle::init(unsigned long rad)
{
        cout << "init: 1 arg\n";
        xorigin = 0;    // default value
        yorigin = 0;    // default value
        radius = rad;
}
```

The output produced is:

```
init: 3 args
init: 2 args
init: 1 arg
```

The definitions of the three versions are essentially the same except for the argument lists. The name mangling typically produces names that include the class name as well as the function name and argument list.

Function overloading works by having different signatures for the same-named function. We also can have two versions of the same function in which both have the same number *and* type of arguments. This is possible if one function is qualified and the other is not, or if they have different qualifiers. For example:

```
#include <iostream.h>

class Circle {
        long xorigin;
        long yorigin;
        unsigned long radius;
public:
        void fun1();
        void fun1() const;
        void fun1() volatile;
        void fun1() const volatile;
};

main()
{
        Circle c1;
        const Circle c2 = c1;
        volatile Circle c3;
        const volatile Circle c4 = c1;

        c1.fun1();      // call non-const non-volatile version
        c2.fun1();      // call const version
        c3.fun1();      // call volatile version
        c4.fun1();      // call const volatile version

        return 0;
}

void Circle::fun1()
{
        cout << "Inside non-const non-volatile version\n";
}
```

```
void Circle::fun1() const
{
        cout << "Inside const version\n";
}

void Circle::fun1() volatile
{
        cout << "Inside volatile version\n";
}

void Circle::fun1() const volatile
{
        cout << "Inside const volatile version\n";
}
```

The output produced is:

```
Inside non-const non-volatile version
Inside const version
Inside volatile version
Inside const volatile version
```

Exercise 2

Overload the `init` function to accept the following sets of arguments:

```
init(year, month, day)
init("dd-Mmm-yyyy")
init(year, julian_day)
init()
```

If no argument is provided, the date to use is Jan 1, 1800.

A Julian day is the day number of the year. For example, Jan 1 is day number 1, Jan 2 is day number 2, and so on. In leap years, day 60 is Feb 29, whereas in non-leap years, it is Mar 1.

Use the standard C library function `atoi` (or `strtol`) to pick off the dd and yyyy parts from a date string.

Don't forget validation.

Default Argument Values

A default value expression may contain terms other than constants. However, there are restrictions on the identifiers permitted there. Specifically, the expression may not contain formal parameters, local variables, or non-`static` member names. Consider the following example:

```
#include <iostream.h>

long val1 = 5;

class Circle {
        long xorigin;
        long yorigin;
        unsigned long radius;
        static unsigned long val2;
public:
        void init(long xo = 0, long yo = val1, unsigned long rad = val2);
        void print(const char *name = "??") const;
};

unsigned long Circle::val2 = 10;
```

The default value expressions reference a global variable and a `static` data member. The values actually used when this function is called are the values those variables have at the time of the call.

Here is the main program:

```
main()
{
        Circle c;

        c.init();
        c.print("c");

        val1 = 20;
        c.init();
        c.print("c");

        return 0;
}
```

The output produced is:

```
Circle c := (0:5:10)
Circle c := (0:20:10)
```

Default Argument Values

In member functions, names in default argument expressions are bound at the end of the class declaration. For example:

```
#include <iostream.h>

int si2;

class test {
        int i;
        static int si1;
public:
        void f(int i1 = si1, int i2 = si2);   // bind to si2 following
        static int si2;
};
```

Here, the si2 referred to in the prototype is the static data member, not the global variable of the same name:

The source continues:

```
int test::si1 = 10;
int test::si2 = 20;

main()
{
        test t;

        t.f();
        test::si2 = 50;
        t.f();

        return 0;
}
void test::f(int i1, int i2)
{
        cout << "i1 = " << i1 << ", i2 = " << i2 << '\n';
}
```

The output produced is:

```
i1 = 10, i2 = 20
i1 = 10, i2 = 50
```

Exercise 3

Extend the `Date` class so that you can specify a print format when calling the `print` function. The formats to implement are as follows:

dd-Mmm-yyyy
dd/mm/yyyy
mm/dd/yyyy
yyyy/mm/dd
yyyy:jul

where jul is the Julian day number (three digits with leading zeros).

The print format argument should have an enumerated type. Its default value should indicate that dates are to be printed in the format dd-Mmm-yyyy.

Inline Member Functions

Inlining Member Functions

Member functions can also be inline. For example:

```
// Inline member functions

class Circle {
        // ...
public:
        inline void init(long xo, long yo, unsigned long rad);
};

inline void Circle::init(long xo, long yo, unsigned long rad)
{
        // ...
}
```

In this case, `inline` may be omitted from the function prototype in the class definition. If `inline` is omitted, `init` is assumed to have external linkage. However, later the compiler comes across an inline definition of that function, so the linkage is changed to internal.

You can achieve the same result in an easier way—by actually writing the definition of the function inside the class definition, as follows:

```
class Circle {
        // ...
public:
        void init(long xo, long yo, unsigned long rad)
        {
                /* code goes here */
        }
};
```

In this case, the `inline` keyword is not needed. Because the member function is defined in the class definition, and the class definition must be in scope whenever objects of its type are declared and used, the code easily can be inlined.

In all member functions we have discussed thus far, we have accessed data members directly by name. As such, any changes to the way in which their data is represented can affect some, if not all, member functions. Consider the case in which a list of valid command strings is stored as a private `static` array of pointers. This was known when the member functions were written and was exploited by using array subscripting to access strings. However, later on, the programmer decided to store the strings in a linked list or perhaps even in a disk file. Now, all direct accesses to that array must be changed.

If we access members only indirectly, for example, through private `Set*` and `Get*` functions (which are often trivial enough that they should be inlined), we can make the program immune from changes in the way in which the private data members are represented. Of course, such changes would require the member access function implementations to be changed accordingly. However, the user interface to those functions would remain the same. The following example contains such a set of functions for the `Circle` class:

```
#include <iostream.h>

class Circle {
        long xorigin;
        long yorigin;
        unsigned long radius;

        long            GetXorigin() const { return xorigin; }
        long            GetYorigin() const { return yorigin; }
        unsigned long   GetRadius()  const { return radius;  }

        void            SetXorigin(long xo)          { xorigin = xo; }
        void            SetYorigin(long yo)          { yorigin = yo; }
        void            SetRadius(unsigned long rad) { radius = rad; }
public:
        void init(long xo = 0, long yo = 0, unsigned long rad = 1);
        void print(const char *name = "??") const;
};
```

By making these functions inline, we reduce them to code that is just as efficient as if we had accessed the members directly.

The code continues:

```
main()
{
        Circle c;

        c.init();
        c.print("c");

        return 0;
}

void Circle::init(long xo, long yo, unsigned long rad)
{
        SetXorigin(xo);
        SetYorigin(yo);
        SetRadius(rad);
}

void Circle::print(const char *name) const
{
        cout << "Circle " << name << " := (" << GetXorigin() << ':'
             << GetYorigin() << ':' << GetRadius()  << ")\n";
}
```

The output produced is:

```
Circle c := (0:0:1)
```

Unfortunately, there is no direct way to prohibit member functions from accessing private members directly. Therefore, if you were converting direct accesses to indirect accesses in an existing program, you could never absolutely be sure you changed all the places necessary, unless you also changed the names of the members being accessed[1]. In the case of the linked list, what used to be an array name might now be a pointer to the first node. If you continue to subscript that name, you will be indexing into some unknown memory location. However, there will not be any compilation errors. On the other hand, if the new access functions access a data file instead, the previously used member names likely will no longer exist, so attempts to access those names directly will be diagnosed.

Another use of Set* and Get* functions involves what in C would be a global variable. For example:

---

[1] Actually, this is a good way to test if you have missed any direct accesses. Change the data members' names and recompile. The only errors you should get are from the new member access functions.

```
#include <iostream.h>

class X {
        static int global;
public:
        static void SetValue(int value) { global = value; }
        static int GetValue()           { return global; }
};

int X::global;
```

In C, global variables are quite often used. In C++, we can put a wrapper around a global and have some control over its access. In this example, class X has only one data member, and that is static. That is, instances of that class contain no data of their own. It is unusual to create an object type while never intending to create objects of that type. (Interestingly, C++ requires that the size of an "empty" class be nonzero.)

Instead of accessing a global variable directly by name, we can access it via a pair of static member functions, as follows:

```
main()
{
        X::SetValue(10);

        cout << X::GetValue() << '\n';
        cout << "sizeof(X) = " << sizeof(X) << '\n';

        return 0;
}
```

Earlier in this section, we discussed the idea of isolating the physical representation of data members from the member functions. To that end, a family of Set* and Get* member access functions was proposed for the Circle class.

In some cases, you can reduce the number of functions by half, by using the same function to both get and set a given "member's" value. While the technique used is interesting, it has severe shortcomings, as we shall see. The approach involves the returning of references, as follows:

```
#include <iostream.h>

class Circle {
        long xorigin;
        long yorigin;
        unsigned long radius;
```

```
        long             & Xorigin() { return xorigin; }
        long             & Yorigin() { return yorigin; }
        unsigned long    & Radius()  { return radius;  }
public:
        Circle(unsigned long rad = 1);
        void print(const char *name = "??");
};
```

Each function returns a reference to the corresponding member, allowing a call to it to be used in the context of both an lvalue and an rvalue, since an access to a reference to an object is exactly the same as an access to the object itself:

```
main()
{
        Circle c;

        c.print("c");
        return 0;
}

Circle::Circle(unsigned long rad)
{
        Xorigin() = 0;
        Yorigin() = 0;
        Radius()  = rad;
}

void Circle::print(const char *name)
{
        cout << "Circle " << name << " := (" << Xorigin() << ':'
             << Yorigin() << ':' << Radius()  << ")\n";
}
```

The output produced is:

```
Circle c := (0:0:1)
```

There is, however, a problem with this particular solution. Until now, the `print` function has been `const`-qualified. That made perfect sense, since it has no need to modify the Circle being passed to it. However, `const`-qualified member functions can call other member functions only if they are like-qualified. In this case they are not, so the calls to them would be rejected. If you then make the three member access functions `const`-qualified to fix this problem, a new problem results. Now these functions are actually returning references to `const` objects, but their return types indicate references to non-`const`. And if you add `const` to the return type, the constructor cannot use them as modifiable lvalues.

At a glance, the approach of using the same function to both get and set a value seems very elegant. However, it has too many shortcomings to be used effectively in robust code. A not-so-obvious problem can occur when the internal representation of a member is changed. For example, consider the case of an array of pointers to strings that is reimplemented as an on-disk file. The set/get function would return some local variable, not the actual record itself, by reference. Thus, when used in a modifiable lvalue context, the private copy, not the record on disk, would be modified. However, if the representation were changed from a file to a linked list, returning a reference to a node member would be just as good as returning a reference to an array element.

Other Issues

A number of other issues are worthy of mention:

- A `friend` function can be inlined.

- Member functions of a local class can be defined only inside the class definition.

- A member function defined inside a class can refer to members following it in the class definition. This is because such function definitions are actually treated by the compiler as if they had followed the class definition in the source.

Exercise 4

Combine the solutions for the previous two exercises into one program. Remove all direct access to the private members **year**, **month**, and **day**, and to the month name and day count arrays. Instead, access these members via a number of **Set*** and **Get*** functions, which are trivial enough that they should be inlined. For example:

```
day_t    GetDay();
month_t  GetMonth();
year_t   GetYear();

void     SetDay(day_t dd);
void     SetMonth(month_t mm);
void     SetYear(year_t yy);

static const char *GetMonthNamesAbbrev(month_t mm);
static day_t GetDaysInMonth(int leapflag, month_t mm);
```

Change the month array definitions so they can be accessed only via these new functions.

Now the program is immune from changes in the way in which the private data members are represented. For example, instead of storing the date as year, month, and day, we could store it as year and Julian day. We could also store the month names in a linked list or even in a disk file. Of course, such changes would require the new member access functions to be changed accordingly.

Chapter 9

Constructors and Destructors

It can be very useful to have a function called automatically each time an object of a class is created. C++ provides such a capability via a special member function called a *constructor*. The main purpose of such a function is to ensure that the object being created is initialized in a predictable value. It also can be useful to have another function called when the object is destroyed or deallocated. Such a function is called a *destructor*.

In this chapter, we will see how to define and use constructors and destructors for our own classes. We will also see how they help make dynamic memory allocation fit more smoothly into the language.

Constructors

The name of a constructor must be the same as its class. For example, any constructor for the class `Circle` must also be called `Circle`. A constructor is called automatically every time an object of its type is created. Consider the following program that creates four Circles, initializes them, and displays their contents:

```
#include <iostream.h>

class Circle {
        long xorigin;
        long yorigin;
        unsigned long radius;
public:
        Circle(long xo, long yo, unsigned long rad = 1);
        Circle(unsigned long rad = 1);
        void print(const char *name = "??") const;
};
```

There are two constructors. Like other member functions, constructors can be overloaded.

Although a constructor looks like and behaves like a `void` function, you cannot explicitly declare it as such; `void` is simply implied.

Here is the main program:

```
main()
{
        Circle c1(3, 5, 2);
        Circle c2(4, 6);
        Circle c3(2);
        Circle c4;              // NOT Circle c4();

        c1.print("c1");
        c2.print("c2");
        c3.print("c3");
        c4.print("c4");

        return 0;
}
```

The declarations for c1, c2, c3, and c4 cause each object created to be initialized using the constructor with the matching argument list. As c4 has no initializer, the *default constructor*—that having no arguments[1]—is called. If constructors are defined but none of them is a default constructor, situations requiring a default constructor will cause a compile-time error to be produced. There is a subtle difference between `Circle c4;` and `Circle c4();`. The first declares c4 to be an object, whereas the second declares it to be a function having no arguments. Beware!

Here are the definitions of the constructors:

```
Circle::Circle(long xo, long yo, unsigned long rad)
{
        xorigin = xo;
        yorigin = yo;
        radius = rad;
}

Circle::Circle(unsigned long rad)
{
        xorigin = 0;
        yorigin = 0;
        radius = rad;
}
```

The output produced is:

---

[1] If all arguments in a constructor have default values, that constructor is also considered to be a default constructor. There can be only one default constructor for a class, however.

```
Circle c1 := (3:5:2)
Circle c2 := (4:6:1)
Circle c3 := (0:0:2)
Circle c4 := (0:0:1)
```

The main purpose of a constructor is to eliminate the age-old problem of forgetting to initialize an object. (Of course, being a function, a constructor can do much more than just give an object a predictable value.) If you do not have an explicit initializer in an object definition, the default constructor is called to provide a guaranteed default initial value.

The syntax used to initialize a structure also can be used to initialize a class object, provided that the class has no constructors and all its data members are public. The class may contain static data members, provided they are public.

An object's initializer can also be an expression. For example:

```
Circle c3 = 2;
```

This is equivalent to:

```
Circle c3(2);
```

This is permitted only if there is a constructor whose one and only argument is compatible with the initializing expression's type. Therefore, constructors having one argument have an extra property: They can convert expressions to the type of their class. Such constructors are called *conversion constructors*, and they automatically will be used when expressions of the appropriate type are found but an object type is expected.

Destructors

Consider the following example in which four objects are created and destroyed on the basis of their scopes in the program. A count of the number of objects in existence at any time is maintained, with its value displayed each time an object is created or destroyed:

```
class Circle {
        long xorigin;
        long yorigin;
        unsigned long radius;
        static unsigned long count;
public:
        Circle();       // constructor
        ~Circle();      // destructor
        void print(const char *name = "??") const;
};

unsigned long Circle::count = 0;
```

The name of a destructor is the name of the class preceded by the tilde (~) character. A destructor can be considered the "complement" of a constructor. As a destructor has no argument list, it cannot be overloaded. And like constructors, destructors cannot be declared with an explicit return type.

Here then is the main program:

```
#include <iostream.h>

main()
{
        Circle c1;                      // c1 start

        c1.print("c1");
        {
                Circle c2;              // c2 start

                c2.print("c2");
                {
                        Circle c3;      // c3 start

                        c3.print("c3");
                }                       // c3 end
        }                               // c2 end

        {
                Circle c4;              // c4 start

                c4.print("c4");
        }                               // c4 end

        return 0;
}                                       // c1 end

Circle::Circle()
{
        xorigin = 0;
        yorigin = 0;
        radius = 1;
        cout << "++ count = " << ++count << '\n';
}

Circle::~Circle()
{
        cout << "-- count = " << --count << '\n';
}
```

The output produced is:

```
++ count = 1
Circle c1 := (0:0:1)
++ count = 2
Circle c2 := (0:0:1)
++ count = 3
Circle c3 := (0:0:1)
-- count = 2
-- count = 1
++ count = 2
Circle c4 := (0:0:1)
-- count = 1
-- count = 0
```

In this example, all objects have automatic storage duration, so conceptually, they come and go at the start and end, respectively, of their parent block. And as shown, the constructor is indeed called at the start of the parent block, and the corresponding destructor is invoked when that block terminates. Standard C does not say when an automatic object is actually created or destroyed; it just says that to try to access it outside its scope results in undefined behavior. Most C compilers, in fact, allocate all automatic data on entry to a function and do not release it until the parent function terminates. This is, of course, an implementation issue that is not affected by C++'s requirements. C++ simply requires any constructor and destructor to be called at the expected place, regardless of how long the object physically exists.

Consider the case of a string class in which each string object is really a descriptor for a string and does not itself contain the text of the string. When such an object is constructed, dynamic memory is allocated to store the text. The corresponding destructor would then free up that memory. Similarly, when a new node is constructed for a linked list, the constructor would insert it in the list and the destructor would remove it.

A constructor or destructor cannot be `static`, `const`, or `volatile`. Despite this, a constructor or destructor can be called for `const`- and `volatile`-qualified objects. They, in turn can also call `const`- and `volatile`-qualified member functions.

An object whose class has a constructor or destructor cannot be a member of a union.

You cannot take the address of a constructor or a destructor.

Aggregates Containing Objects

As you might expect, you can have an array of objects of class `Circle`. Also, objects can be nested inside structures, unions, and other classes. An array of Circles is declared just as in C. The interesting issue, though, is the initializer format. For example:

```
// Circle class definition goes here

const int size = 6;
```

```
main()
{
        Circle c[size] = {
                Circle(1, 2, 3),
                Circle(1, 2),
                Circle(2),
                4
        };

        int i;
        char text[10];

        for (i = 0; i < size; ++i) {
                sprintf(text, "c[%d]", i);
                c[i].print(text);
        }

        return 0;
}
```

The output produced is:

```
Circle c[0] := (1:2:3)
Circle c[1] := (1:2:1)
Circle c[2] := (0:0:2)
Circle c[3] := (0:0:4)
Circle c[4] := (0:0:1)
Circle c[5] := (0:0:1)
```

In Standard C, all expressions in an initializer for an aggregate must be constant expressions, even those for automatic objects. This is not true in C++. Clearly, a constructor is a function that must be called at run time. When you use the constructor approach to initialize an object, C++ permits nonconstant expressions. How then are the initializer expressions handled, and what are the default values used for the last two elements? The first three expressions map into three distinct constructors, according to their argument list. And as we saw earlier, expression 4 is equivalent to `Circle(4)`, which results in a call to the constructor with one argument. The unspecified elements take on the value provided by the default constructor. In C, they take on a value of zero.

Initializing Reference and const Members

A class member may be a reference to another object so that all operations on that member actually take place on the object to which it is referenced. A class data member may also be `const`-qualified. However, to initialize reference or `const`-qualified members we need a slightly different approach, because we cannot assign to such members directly in a constructor.

Initializing Reference and const Members

The approach needed is as follows. Although references are not used in the example, the same rules apply:

```
#include <iostream.h>

class Circle {
        long xorigin;
        long yorigin;
        const unsigned long radius;      // const-qualified
public:
        Circle(long xo, long yo, unsigned long rad = 1);
        void print(const char *name = "??") const;
};

main()
{
        Circle c(5, 10, 15);

        c.print("c");

        return 0;
}

Circle::Circle(long xo, long yo, unsigned long rad) : radius(rad)
{                                                    // ∼∼∼∼∼∼∼∼∼∼
        xorigin = xo;
        yorigin = yo;
}
```

The output produced is:

```
Circle c := (5:10:15)
```

Note the new construct after the function argument list but before the body of the constructor. The colon introduces a comma-separated list of expressions that are evaluated before the body of the constructor is entered. Each expression must have the form:

member-name (initial-value)

In this case, `radius(rad)` causes the const-qualified member `radius` to be initialized with the value `rad`. You also can use this notation for the other members, even though it is not necessary to do so. For example, you could define the constructor as follows:

```
Circle::Circle(long xo, long yo, unsigned long rad)
 : radius(rad), xorigin(xo), yorigin(yo)
{
}
```

These special initializers are evaluated in the order of occurrence of the data members in the class definition, not in the order in which they are written in the constructor definition. That is, the commas are punctuators, not operators.

A nonstatic `const` array member cannot be initialized in this or any other way, however.

Constructors in Nested Classes

We have seen that classes may nest. And since each class can have constructors and a destructor, it is important to understand the order of execution of these functions. For example:

```
#include <iostream.h>

class Circle {
        long xorigin;
        long yorigin;
        unsigned long radius;
public:
        Circle(long xo = 1, long yo = 2, unsigned long rad = 3);
        ~Circle();
        void print(const char *name = "??") const;
};

class Rectangle {
        long xorigin;
        long yorigin;
        unsigned long xlen;
        unsigned long ylen;
public:
        Rectangle(long xo = 4, long yo = 5,
                  unsigned long xl = 6, unsigned long yl = 7);
        ~Rectangle();
        void print(const char *name = "??") const;
};

class Group {
        Circle c1;
        Rectangle r[2];
        Circle c2;
        int i;
public:
```

```
                Group(int = 8);
                ~Group();
                void print(const char *name = "??") const;
        };

        main()
        {
                Group g;

                g.print("g");

                return 0;
        }

        Circle::Circle(long xo, long yo, unsigned long rad)
        {
                cout << "In Circle constructor\n";
                xorigin = xo;
                yorigin = yo;
                radius = rad;
        }

        Circle::~Circle()
        {
                cout << "In Circle destructor\n";
        }

        Rectangle::Rectangle(long xo, long yo, unsigned long xl, unsigned long yl)
        {
                cout << "In Rectangle constructor\n";
                xorigin = xo;
                yorigin = yo;
                xlen = xl;
                ylen = yl;
        }

        Rectangle::~Rectangle()
        {
                cout << "In Rectangle destructor\n";
        }
```

```
Group::Group(int value)
{
        cout << "In Group constructor\n";
        i = value;
}

Group::~Group()
{
        cout << "In Group destructor\n";
}

void Circle::print(const char *name) const
{
        cout << "Circle " << name << " := (" << xorigin << ':'
             << yorigin << ':' << radius  << ")\n";
}

void Rectangle::print(const char *name) const
{
        cout << "Rectangle " << name << " := (" << xorigin << ':'
             << yorigin << ':' << xlen << ':' << ylen << ")\n";
}

void Group::print(const char *name) const
{
        cout << "Group " << name << " := {\n";
        c1.print("c1");
        r[0].print("r[0]");
        r[1].print("r[1]");
        c2.print("c2");
        cout << "i := " << i << "\n}\n";
}
```

The output produced is:

```
In Circle constructor
In Rectangle constructor
In Rectangle constructor
In Circle constructor
In Group constructor
Group g := {
Circle c1 := (1:2:3)
Rectangle r[0] := (4:5:6:7)
Rectangle r[1] := (4:5:6:7)
```

Static Data and Execution Order

```
        Circle c2 := (1:2:3)
        i := 8
        }
        In Group destructor
        In Circle destructor
        In Rectangle destructor
        In Rectangle destructor
        In Circle destructor
```

The ordering is quite intuitive. First, the nested object constructors are called in member order. Then the nonnested members are initialized. And finally, the destructors are called in the reverse order.

Static Data and Execution Order

Thus far, all of the objects used with constructors have had automatic storage class, and it is clear when such objects are created and destroyed. But what about static objects? If they really are created at compile or link time, what is the order of evaluation of their constructors and destructors?

The following example contains global Circles, **static** Circles with file scope, and automatic and **static** Circles with block scope. The output shows the order in which the constructors and destructors are called:

```
#include <iostream.h>

class Circle {
        long xorigin;
        long yorigin;
        unsigned long radius;
public:
        Circle(unsigned long rad = 1);
        ~Circle();
};

void test1();
void test2();

static Circle c1(1), c2(2);
Circle c3(3);
static Circle c4(4);

main()
{
```

```
                Circle c5(5);
                static Circle c6(6), c7(7);
                Circle c8(8), c9(9);
                static Circle c10(10);



                {
                        static Circle c11(11);
                        {
                                Circle c12(12);

                                test1();
                        }
                }
                {
                        Circle c13(13);
                }

                return 0;
        }

        Circle c14(14), c15(15);

        void test1()
        {
                Circle c16(16);
                static Circle c17(17);

                {
                        Circle c18(18);
                }
        }

        void test2()
        {
                Circle c19(19);
                static Circle c20(20);
        }

        Circle::Circle(unsigned long rad)
        {
                radius = rad;
                cout << "++ " << radius << '\n';
        }
```

Static Data and Execution Order

```
Circle::~Circle()
{
        cout << "-- " << radius << '\n';
}
```

The output produced is as follows. It is arranged in tabular form simply to save space. Read down each column, left to right:

Part 1	Part 2	Part 3	Part 4
++ 1	++ 8	-- 16	-- 10
++ 2	++ 9	-- 12	-- 7
++ 3	++ 10	++ 13	-- 6
++ 4	++ 11	-- 13	-- 15
++ 14	++ 12	-- 9	-- 14
++ 15	++ 16	-- 8	-- 4
++ 5	++ 17	-- 5	-- 3
++ 6	++ 18	-- 17	-- 2
++ 7	-- 18	-- 11	-- 1

To make the output easier to follow, the radius of each Circle created is the same number used in that variable's name. For example, c6 is initialized with 6, c10 with 10, and so on.

The rules for calling constructors and destructors for static objects are as follows:

- Constructors for nonlocal statics (c1 through c4 and c14 through c15) are called in their lexical order within the source module. The initialization of any nonlocal statics in a source module is performed before the first use of any function or object defined in that module. The corresponding destructors are called in the reverse order when **main** returns or when **exit** is called and **atexit** functions have completed.

- Constructors for local statics (c6, c7, c10, c11, and c17) are called the first time execution passes through their declarations. The corresponding destructors are called in the reverse order either just before or as part of **atexit** processing. Note that function **test2** is not called. Execution never drops through the local static 20. Consequently, its constructor and destructor are never called (likewise for 19).

A similar situation occurs with aggregate initializers. For example, the following program shows the order in which constructors and destructors are called for the six elements in a two-dimensional array:

```
#include <iostream.h>

class Circle {
        long xorigin;
        long yorigin;
        unsigned long radius;
public:
        Circle(unsigned long rad = 1);
        ~Circle();
};

main()
{
        Circle c[][2] = {
                {Circle(1), Circle(2)},
                {Circle(3), Circle(4)},
                {Circle(5), Circle(6)}
        };

        return 0;
}
```

The output produced is:

```
++  1
++  2
++  3
++  4
++  5
++  6
--  6
--  5
--  4
--  3
--  2
--  1
```

As you might expect on the basis of the previous discussion of ordering, the elements are initialized in lexical order and destroyed in the reverse order.

We have learned about the ordering within a program built from a single source file. However, real programs are made up from multiple source modules, each of which may contain static and automatic data declarations. How does that affect the order in which constructors and destructors are called? Just how does the executable program know which static constructors and destructors to call? The compiler sees only one source module at a time. The answer is that no ordering is imposed *across* source modules.

The Effects of Changing Control Flow

There are a number of ways of bypassing the normal flow of control in a program. You can use the statements **break**, **continue**, **goto**, and **switch**, or the library functions **exit**, **abort**, or **longjmp**. These statements and functions unconditionally transfer control to some other place in the program and, in the process, bypass the usual block termination. Will destructors be called for objects in existence at the time of such a statement or function call? Consider the following program:

```
#include <iostream.h>
#include <stdlib.h>

class Circle {
        long xorigin;
        long yorigin;
        unsigned long radius;
public:
        Circle(unsigned long rad = 1);
        ~Circle();
};

main()
{
        Circle c1(1);
        int i;

        for (i = 1; i < 4; ++i) {
                Circle c2(2);

                if (i == 2) {
                        break;
                }
        }

        exit(0);
        return 0;
}

Circle::Circle(unsigned long rad)
{
        radius = rad;
        cout << "++ " << radius << '\n';
}
```

```
Circle::~Circle()
{
        cout << "-- " << radius << '\n';
}
```

The output produced is:

```
++ 1
++ 2
-- 2
++ 2
-- 2
```

A new c2 object is created and destroyed for each iteration of the loop, as you would expect. The **break** forces destructors to be called for automatic objects in the block(s) from which it breaks out. The same is true for **goto** and **continue**, although they are not present in this example.

Calling **exit** directly, or indirectly by returning from **main**, causes destructors to be called for static objects only. Hence, no destructor is called for c1[2]. A direct call to **exit** is like a return from **main** only if the following condition exists: The call to **exit** is located such that none of its parent blocks, or blocks in functions that are calling this function, have automatic objects with destructors defined.

abort does not invoke destructors at all, which is in keeping with **abort**'s purpose. By trapping SIGABRTs using the **signal** function, you could intercept them and call **exit** yourself. (This would be useful if you use the **assert.h** macro **assert** in debugging. This macro expands to a call to **abort** when NDEBUG is not defined.)

The setjmp/longjmp facility also behaves as you might expect. When longjmp restores to some previous context, all automatic objects created since that context was saved are destroyed. However, no destructors are called on their behalf, since their parent blocks are terminated abnormally. Beware!

In C, **goto** and **switch** allow control to jump into a block, bypassing the initializers of automatic objects. C++ does not permit initializers to be bypassed.

If a program terminates, and memory allocated with **new** was not explicitly **delete**d, it is unspecified whether the corresponding destructors, if any, are automatically invoked.

Temporary Objects

A constructor can be called directly to create a temporary, unnamed object. For example:

```
f(Circle(1, 2, 3), Circle(7, 8, 9))
```

Here, the constructor is called directly to create two Circles that are initialized as shown.

---

[2]The draft C++ standard includes support for exception handling. Part of this machinery can cause cleanup of automatic objects across a call to **exit**.

Dynamically Allocated Objects

The temporary objects are then passed to f and then are destroyed automatically. This avoids creating named temporaries.

Temporary objects are also created and destroyed—and therefore, require corresponding constructors and destructors to be called—under other circumstances. Examples include when objects are passed to, and returned from, functions by value and when an object is created as the result of an explicit or implicit cast.

The lifetime of a temporary object is typically quite short—no longer than the life of its parent expression. An expression that causes more than one temporary object to be created will destroy them in the reverse order of their creation, whatever that may have been.

Dynamically Allocated Objects

A big advantage of new and delete comes with classes having constructors and/or destructors. If an object created by new is to behave just like an object created using an automatic or static definition, new and delete must involve implicit calls to constructors and destructors. And this is, in fact, the case. For example:

```
#include <iostream.h>
#include <stdlib.h>

class Circle {
        long xorigin;
        long yorigin;
        unsigned long radius;
public:
        void print(const char *name = "??") const;
        Circle();
        ~Circle();
};

main()
{
        Circle *pcir1, *pcir2;

/*1*/   pcir1 = new Circle;
        if (pcir1 == 0) {
                cout << "pcir1 allocation failure\n";
                exit(1);
        }

/*2*/   pcir1->print("pcir1");
```

```
/*3*/   pcir2 = new Circle [3];
        if (pcir2 == 0) {
                cout << "pcir2 allocation failure\n";
                exit(1);
        }

        pcir2[0].print("pcir2[0]");
        pcir2[1].print("pcir2[1]");
        pcir2[2].print("pcir2[2]");

/*4*/   delete pcir1;
/*5*/   delete [] pcir2;

        return 0;
}
```

In case 1, we allocated a single Circle using **new Circle**. Because a default constructor is defined, it is called, resulting in the object being initialized with an origin of (0,0) and radius 1.

The expression `pcir1->print("pcir1")` in case 2 is new but not surprising. Thus far, we have called member functions using a class object's name. However, in this case we do not know its name; we only know its address, so we use the **->** operator to select the **print** member function for class **Circle** to operate on the Circle pointed to by **pcir1**.

In case 3, we allocate an array of three Circles using **new Circle [3]**, which results in the default constructor being called for each element in ascending order, just as if the array had been declared automatic or static.

The **delete** statements in cases 4 and 5 cause the single Circle to be freed first, followed by the array of three Circles, in descending order of subscript:

```
Circle::Circle()
{
        cout << "** In constructor\n";
        xorigin = 0;
        yorigin = 0;
        radius  = 1;
}

Circle::~Circle()
{
        cout << "++ In destructor\n";
}
```

The output produced is:

Dynamically Allocated Objects

```
** In constructor
Circle pcir1 := (0:0:1)
** In constructor
** In constructor
** In constructor
Circle pcir2[0] := (0:0:1)
Circle pcir2[1] := (0:0:1)
Circle pcir2[2] := (0:0:1)
++ In destructor
++ In destructor
++ In destructor
++ In destructor
```

Initialization

As demonstrated in the previous example, the default constructor, if any, is used to initialize an object of a given class. For example, in the code above, the expression:

```
pcir = new Circle
```

causes the object to be initialized as follows:

```
** In constructor
Circle *pcir := (0:0:1)
++ In destructor
```

An optional part of the syntax of new is an initializer. For example:

```
pcir = new Circle ()
```

has an empty initializer list, indicating that the default constructor should be used. It is equivalent to having no initializer at all. If a constructor with three arguments is defined as follows:

```
Circle::Circle(long xo, long yo, unsigned long rad)
{
        cout << "** In non-default constructor\n";
        xorigin = xo;
        yorigin = yo;
        radius  = rad;
}
```

the expression:

```
pcir = new Circle (3, 4, 5)
```

causes the object to be initialized as follows:

```
** In non-default constructor
Circle *pcir := (3:4:5)
++ In destructor
```

Finally, the initializer can be an expression of the appropriate class type rather than an initializer list:

```
main()
{
        Circle *pcir;
        Circle cir;

        cir.print("cir");

/*1*/   pcir = new Circle (cir);
        if (pcir == 0) {
                cout << "pcir allocation failure\n";
                exit(1);
        }

        pcir->print("*pcir");

        delete pcir;

        return 0;
}
```

The output produced is:

```
** In constructor
Circle cir := (0:0:1)
Circle *pcir := (0:0:1)
++ In destructor
++ In destructor
```

The automatic object `cir` is created, and the default constructor is called to initialize it. In case 1, the expression `pcir = new Circle (cir)` causes a Circle to be allocated at run time, but the default constructor is *not* called. Instead, the object is initialized to have the same value as `cir`. Specifically, then, the constructor is called once while the corresponding destructor is called twice.

Arrays cannot be initialized explicitly when using **new**. Each element of an array can, however, be initialized to the same value by using a default constructor, as shown earlier.

String Class Example

Thus far, class objects have been self-contained. That is, all data belonging to that object has been stored inside that object. For many classes, an object might store a pointer to the real data rather than contain the data itself. One such example would be a String class. For example:

```
#include <iostream.h>
#include <string.h>

class String {
        unsigned length;
        char *ptext;
public:
        String(const char *pc = 0);
        ~String();
};
```

A String contains a length and a pointer to the first character in the string. However, there is no room in the object for the text of the string—only a descriptor for it. You allocate space for the text by using **new**. That is, a String object simply describes a string but does not actually contain one.

The String member functions follow:

```
String::String(const char *pc)
{
        cout << "In constructor\n";
        if (pc == 0) {          // string is empty
                length = 0;
                ptext = 0;
        }
        else {
                length = strlen(pc);
                ptext = new char [length + 1];
                strcpy(ptext, pc);
        }
}

String::~String()
{
        cout << "In destructor\n";
        if (ptext != 0) {       // if string not empty delete it
                delete [] ptext;
                ptext = 0;
                length = 0;
        }
}
```

Vector and matrix classes are commonly implemented in the same manner.

User-Defined Versions of new and delete

Each time we have used new or delete in the examples above, the standard library functions underlying new and delete were used. However, users can provide their own versions by overloading these operators. (This is detailed in chapter 1, "Operator Overloading.") Because operators are overloaded on a per-class basis, you can define custom implementations for new and delete on a per-class basis.

If user-defined versions of new and delete exist, you can still access the standard implementations by prefixing these keywords with the :: scope resolution operator as in Circle pcir = ::new Circle; and ::delete pcir;.

Exercise 5

Turn the date init functions, written in earlier exercises, into constructors. This allows an object to be initialized at the time it is created.

Define a 3 × 2 array of dates and initialize the first column only, with the dates for yesterday, today, and tomorrow. Print the contents of *all* the elements. Define a new constructor as follows:

```
Date(relday ytt);
```

where ytt can be any one of the three enumeration constants yesterday, today, or tomorrow from the relative day enumerated type relday.

Use the time.h functions time and localtime to get today's date.

The function time determines the current calendar time. It is used as follows:

```
#include <time.h>

time_t time(time_t *timer);
```

The encoding of the type time_t is unspecified. The returned value is an approximation of the current calendar time. If this time is not available, (time_t)(-1) is returned. If timer is not 0, the return value is also assigned to the object pointed to by timer.

The function localtime converts the calendar time pointed to by timer into a broken-down time, expressed as local time:

```
#include <time.h>

struct tm *localtime(const time_t *timer);
```

The value returned points to the broken-down time object.

The `time.h` structure type `tm` contains the individual components of a calendar time. Collectively, they are known as the broken-down time. The following members must be present in the structure, in any order. Other implementation-defined members also may be present:

```
struct tm {
        int  tm_sec;    seconds after midnight [0, 61]
        int  tm_min;    minutes after the hour [0, 59]
        int  tm_hour;   hours since midnight [0, 23]
        int  tm_mday;   day of the month [1, 31]
        int  tm_mon;    months since January [0, 11]
        int  tm_year;   years since 1900
        int  tm_wday;   days since Sunday [0, 6]
        int  tm_yday;   days since January 1 [0, 365]
        int  tm_isdst;  daylight saving time flag
};
```

where:

```
tm_isdst >  0   daylight savings in effect
         == 0   daylight savings not in effect
         <  0   information not available
```

Exercise 6

Revise the constructor `Date("dd-Mmm-yyyy")` by using string decoding instead of `atoi/strtol` to pick off dd and yyyy. Test the constructor on a few dates.

Exercise 7

Define two public member functions called `MinDate` and `MaxDate` that compare two dates and return the minimum or maximum one, respectively, by value.

Chapter 10

Operator Overloading

The addition of classes is a step toward integrating user-defined types into the language. Once a class has been defined, we can create objects of that type by using the same notation as C++'s built-in types. However, to make these classes really fit in, we need to be able to operate on class objects, using the same easy notation allowed by the built-in operators.

In this chapter, we will see how most of the built-in operators can be overloaded for class objects.

Introduction to Operator Overloading

Consider the case of a structure describing a complex number type. The structure would contain two members, one for the real part and the other for the imaginary part, as follows:

```
typedef struct {
        float real;
        float imag;
} Complex;

Complex c1, c2, c3;
```

In C, to add two complex numbers together, we have to revert to something such as the following:

```
c1 = addcomplex(c2, c3);
```

Declaring the type and allocating the `Complex` variables is not a problem. However, because there is no way to describe how to perform an addition operation on two complex numbers, we have to revert to function calls to do even the most basic arithmetic. No matter how we do it, `Complex` still is obviously not a base type, and it does not really fit into the language. So we must translate the intuitive notation that a mathematician might use with complex arithmetic into some not-so-intuitive scheme to implement the solution. What we would really prefer is the following:

```
c1 = c2 + c3;
```

C++ allows this. You can assign meaning to almost all of its built-in operators when they are used in the context of a user-defined type. In this case, we can define what + means when its operands have type Complex. Assigning an alternative meaning to existing operators is called *operator overloading*.

For mathematical classes such as complex arithmetic, vectors, and matrices, most of the built-in arithmetic operators immediately become candidates for overloading. And while you can define c1 - c2 to actually produce a sum, that would be counterintuitive. That is, you must take care that the operator symbol you choose for a particular meaning implies some reasonable meaning. Which operator, for example, would you choose to invert a matrix? None of the built-in operators implies such an operation, so you would be forced to choose one that is obscure. Also, you should try to be consistent. If you make % mean completely different things for different classes, it would be very hard to understand the resulting expressions that use that operator. Just when does it mean the usual modulus and when is it one of the (possibly obscure) overloaded uses?

All operators maintain the precedence assigned to them in the language definition, whether or not they are overloaded. For example, the binary * and / operators always have higher precedence than the binary + and - operators. Similarly, the associativity of operators with the same precedence is preserved. Another reasonable restriction is that overloaded operators must have the same number of operands as their built-in counterparts. And they cannot have default arguments.

Four operators cannot be overloaded: ., .*, ::, and ?:.

With C and C++'s built-in types, we have come to learn certain rules. For example:

- Certain expressions are commutative (for example, a + b ≡ b + a).
- i++, ++i, i += 1, and i = i + 1 are related.
- a[i] ≡ *(a + i)

However, once you start to overload operators, none of these guarantees is automatically preserved.

A few operators are predefined for all types, including classes. These are simple assignment (=), address-of (&), indirect member selection (->), and comma (,). In any event, if you can come up with a good reason, these can be overloaded on a per-class basis also.

Another aspect to consider is the type of the result of certain operators. The built-in relational and equality operators (among others) produce a result of type int with value 0 (false) or 1 (true). And while this is a useful thing to imitate (for example, in overloading them for a Complex or Vector class), it is not required.

Similarly, many built-in operators expect operands of specific types, and if their operands are not the expected type but are compatible types, they are promoted before being operated on. This is not promised for overloaded versions.

Some Simple Examples

We will begin by overloading the equality operators == and != when both operands are objects of type `Circle`:

```
#include <iostream.h>

class Circle {
        long xorigin;
        long yorigin;
        unsigned long radius;
public:
        Circle(long xo, long yo, unsigned long rad = 1);

        int operator==(const Circle &c) const   // overload == operator
        {
                return ((c.xorigin == xorigin) &&
                        (c.yorigin == yorigin) &&
                        (c.radius == radius));
        }

        int operator!=(const Circle &c) const   // overload != operator
        {
                return !(c == *this);
        }
};
```

To overload an operator for a particular class, you must specify a special member function in that class definition. And because we need to be able to access these overloaded operators from outside member functions, these special functions must be `public`.

To overload an operator, we must use the keyword `operator`, as shown above. In the first case, we specify that we wish to overload the == operator. Since this is a binary operator, we must specify the types of both its operands. However, we have only shown one argument, of type `Circle`. This is the type of the right operand. The type of the left operand is automatically assumed to be an object of the class being defined. The type of the result produced is indicated by the function return type.

If these operator functions are designed to behave just like their built-in operator counterparts, we can use these new versions in the same manner. For example:

```
main()
{
        Circle c1(1, 2, 4);
        Circle c2(1, 2, 4);
        Circle c3(4, -2, 4);
```

```
    cout << "c1 == c2 => " << (c1 == c2) << '\n';
    cout << "c1 != c2 => " << (c1 != c2) << '\n';
    cout << "c1 == c3 => " << (c1 == c3) << '\n';
    cout << "c1 != c3 => " << (c1 != c3) << '\n';

    return 0;
}
```

Three Circles are created, two of which have identical properties. If the overloaded operators produce an `int` result with value 0 or 1 like their built-in counterparts, we can reasonably expect the following output:

```
c1 == c2 => 1
c1 != c2 => 0
c1 == c3 => 0
c1 != c3 => 1
```

and that is what results.

The operator overload functions are quite simple. In the case of the `==` function, we need to compare each of the three members for the two Circles. Because the left operand is passed in as a hidden argument, we do not need to refer to it by name. Instead, we simply access its members by name just as we do in other member functions. On the other hand, the right argument must be given a formal parameter name, and we must use that to refer to that object's members.

We can see how easy and intuitive it becomes to compare two Circles. The expression `c1 == c2` says it all. However, what is really happening behind the scenes is that the `==` operator function is being called to produce a value that is then used in place of the expression.

Note how the `!=` is defined in terms of the `==` operator. This is a common approach when operators have related behavior. For example, `<=` can be defined in terms of `>`. Not only does it require less coding; it also means that one less member function need know about the private internals of the class.

Passing a potentially large class object by value can be expensive and is generally unnecessary, as is passing a structure by value. Coming from C, we may be inclined to pass the arguments by address. And while that could perhaps be made to work, it would require us to explicitly anticipate this by using the `&` operator when the operands are passed. The far better approach is to pass by reference, since this requires no special notification other than in the function prototype.

As we have passed a reference to the right operand, we could get at that underlying object and even modify it. But because it is reasonable to expect that `==` will not modify its operands, we should protect them as much as possible. This is why we have the `const` qualifier.

The `const` function qualifiers cause `this` to be passed as a pointer to a `const` object instead of as a pointer to non-`const` object. As a result, we are prohibited from modifying the left argument as well.

A commonly used alternative to `const`-qualifying the functions is to use a **friend** function, as follows:

```
friend int operator==(const Circle &c1, const Circle &c2);
```

While this approach works, it seems a little strange to force the operator to live outside the `Circle` class. After all, it can be used only with objects of that class anyway.

Always declare operator functions `const` unless the operator being overloaded is expected to somehow modify its left (or only) operand as a side effect. And as we have seen, passing other operands by reference and with the `const` qualifier is efficient as well as safe.

Exercise 8

Define the following operators for `Date` objects so that they behave in the same manner as their built-in counterparts: ==, !=, <, <=, >, and >=.

List Class

Until now, we have dealt exclusively with the `Circle` class. We will now introduce another simple class that contains an array of elements. As well as providing some variety, this new class lets us develop some more interesting overloaded operator functions. For example, it makes sense to perform numerous arithmetic operations on lists of integers, whereas the operations we might want to perform on Circles are more limited. Our very simple list class is limited to arrays of three integers. If we were designing a general-purpose vector package, we would want to handle lists of variable length. However, that is more complicated than we need for now.

For our new class, we define that adding an integer to a List produces a new List in which all the previous List's elements have been incremented by the integer amount. Let us then define an operator function to overload addition:

```
#include <iostream.h>

class List {
        int elem[3];
public:
        List(int e0 = 0, int e1 = 0, int e2 = 0);
        void print(const char *name = "??") const;

        List operator+(int i) const;
};
```

The operator function expects a List as its left operand and an `int` as its right operand:

```
main()
{
        List list1(3, 6, 0);
        List list2;

        list1.print("list1");
/*1*/   list2 = list1 + 3;
        list2.print("list2");
/*2*/   list2 = list1 + 3.75;
        list2.print("list2");
/*3*/   list2 = list1 + 3.75 + 3.75;
        list2.print("list2");
/*4*/   list2 = list1 + 7.5;
        list2.print("list2");

        return 0;
}
```

The `print` member function displays the List members in the format [xx:yy:zz], and the output produced is as follows:

```
List list1 => [3:6:0]
List list2 => [6:9:3]
List list2 => [6:9:3]
List list2 => [9:12:6]
List list2 => [10:13:7]
```

Case 1 is straightforward; 3 is added to each element in `list1` to produce the list [6:9:3]. `list1` is not modified. In case 2, the right operand has type `double`, and since there is only one operator function defined for addition, the compiler looks to see if that function can be used. The right operand does not match the expected type exactly. However, the two types are assignment-compatible, so the operator function is called with the `double` argument's being converted and passed as an `int`. As a result, we get the same answer as in case 1.

In case 3, we have two addition operators, and they associate left to right. Therefore, the value 3.75 is converted to an `int` and added to `list1`, and the result is then added to another converted value 3, resulting in a List being incremented by 6 all told.

Now while cases 3 and 4 seem to be equivalent at a glance, they are not. In case 4, 7 is added to the List, whereas in case 3, 6 is added. To make case 3 the same as 4, we would need to write it as:

```
/*3*/   list2 = list1 + (3.75 + 3.75);
```

Here then are the member functions:

```
List::List(int e0, int e1, int e2)
{
        elem[0] = e0;
        elem[1] = e1;
        elem[2] = e2;
}

void List::print(const char *name) const
{
        cout << "List " << name << " => [" << elem[0]
             << ":" << elem[1] << ":" << elem[2] << "]\n";
}

List List::operator+(int i) const
{
        List temp;

        temp.elem[0] = elem[0] + i;
        temp.elem[1] = elem[1] + i;
        temp.elem[2] = elem[2] + i;

        return temp;
}
```

The creation of the temporary object causes the constructor to be called, even though we immediately initialize that object in the statements that follow. The destructor (if any) is also called prior to the function's termination.

A slightly different version of the operator function copies the left operand to the temporary and increments each element by the scalar amount:

```
List List::operator+(int i) const
{
        List temp = *this;

        temp.elem[0] += i;
        temp.elem[1] += i;
        temp.elem[2] += i;

        return temp;
}
```

This avoids the constructor being called but requires a List object to be copied. The destructor is still called.

A more interesting solution involves creating an unnamed temporary by explicitly calling the constructor. For example:

```
List List::operator+(int i) const
{
        return List(elem[0] + i, elem[1] + i, elem[2] + i);
}
```

Here we call the constructor to create an unnamed List with an initial value as specified in the argument list. The constructor produces a List that is immediately returned back to the caller by value. All three versions do about the same amount of work. However, the third one is by far the simplest to read and write.

Our operator function is declared using:

```
List operator+(int i) const;
```

and that works fine for the expressions so far. However, look what happens in the following case:

```
list2 = 3 + list1;
```

The compiler rejects this construct because it only knows about having a List as the left operand and an int as the right. So while addition is commutative when used with built-in types, if we want that same property with user-defined classes we have to make it so. We can achieve that by having another overloaded addition function, but this time it must be a **friend** of the class since the left operand is not a class type.

```
class List {
        int elem[3];
public:
...
        List operator+(int i) const;
        friend List operator+(int i, const List &list);
};

main()
{
        List list1(3, 6, 0);
        List list2;

        list1.print("list1");
        list2 = 4 + list1 + 3;
        list2.print("list2");

        return 0;
}
```

```
List List::operator+(int i) const
{
        return List(elem[0] + i, elem[1] + i, elem[2] + i);
}

List operator+(int i, const List &list)
{
        return list + i;
}
```

The expression 4 + list1 + 3 is grouped as ((4 + list1) + 3), which results in both operator functions being called. The output produced is:

```
List list1 => [3:6:0]
List list2 => [10:13:7]
```

We have defined the **friend** function in a clever way by calling the other operator function with the operands reversed. This is commonly done when you implement operators that are commutative.

Let's look at how we might overload the += operator:

```
#include <iostream.h>

class List {
        int elem[3];
public:
        List(int e0 = 0, int e1 = 0, int e2 = 0);
        void print(const char *name = "*name = "??") const;

        List operator+=(int i);
        List operator+(int i) const;
};

main()
{
        List list1(3, 6, 0);
        List list2;

        list1.print("list1");
        list2 = list1 += 3;
        list1.print("list1");
        list2.print("list2");

        return 0;
}
```

```
List List::operator+=(int i)
{
        return *this = *this + i;
}
```

The output produced is:

```
List list1 => [3:6:0]
List list1 => [6:9:3]
List list2 => [6:9:3]
```

This operator results in the left operand's being modified, and its new value becomes the value of the expression. As `this` is a pointer to the left operand, `*this` is the left operand, and so the function cannot be `const`-qualified.

Note how the += operator is implemented in terms of the + operator.

Because of their size, it may well be inefficient to return class objects by value. We could make the operator function += return a reference to a `const` List instead. That can easily be done for this operator, but for others, it takes more work, as we shall see.

Overloading Unary Operators

The unary operators all use prefix notation. Strictly speaking, postfix ++ and --, as well as ( ) and [ ], are called primary, not unary, operators. However, we will discuss them here as well. Unary operators are quite easy to overload. To demonstrate this, we overload the unary minus:

```
class List {
        int elem[3];
public:
...
        List operator-() const;
};

main()
{
        List list1(3, 6, 0);
        List list2;

        list1.print("list1");
        list2 = -list1;
        list2.print("list2");

        return 0;
}
```

Overloading Unary Operators

```
        List List::operator-() const
        {
                return List(-elem[0], -elem[1], -elem[2]);
        }
```

The output produced is:

```
List list1 => [3:6:0]
List list2 => [-3:-6:0]
```

Earlier, we stated that it might be more efficient to return objects by reference. That could be done for this operator, but it would require a static local List to be defined. For a function to return a reference, the object to which the reference refers must exist beyond the life of the function call. That is not the case when an unnamed temporary List is created by the constructor in the example above.

Overloading the prefix versions of ++ and -- is also straightforward:

```
class List {
        int elem[3];
public:
        List(int e0 = 0, int e1 = 0, int e2 = 0);
        void print(const char *name = "??") const;

        List operator++();        // prefix version
        List operator+(int i) const;
};

main()
{
        List list1(3, 6, 0);
        List list2;

        list1.print("list1");
        list2 = ++list1;
        list1.print("list1");
        list2.print("list2");

        return 0;
}

List List::operator++()
{
        return *this = *this + 1;
}
```

The output produced is:

```
List list1 => [3:6:0]
List list1 => [4:7:1]
List list2 => [4:7:1]
```

As you should expect, you can distinguish between prefix and postfix versions of ++ and --. The postfix versions of ++ and -- requires the operator function to have an `int` argument that is set to zero when a postfix operator is encountered. You do not need to ever use this `int` argument, however; it exists simply so there are two distinct signatures for the prefix and postfix operator functions. For example:

```
class List {
        int elem[3];
public:
        List(int e0 = 0, int e1 = 0, int e2 = 0);
        void print(const char *name = "??") const;

        List operator++(int dummy);      // postfix version
        List operator+(int i) const;
};

main()
{
        List list1(3, 6, 0);
        List list2;

        list1.print("list1");
        list2 = list1++;
        list1.print("list1");
        list2.print("list2");

        return 0;
}

List List::operator++(int dummy)
{
        List temp = *this;

        *this = *this + 1;
        return temp;                 // return old value
}
```

The output produced is:

```
List list1 => [3:6:0]
List list1 => [4:7:1]
List list2 => [3:6:0]
```

Exercise 9

Define the following operators for `Date` objects:

Expression Form	Result
Date + *integer*	new date
integer + Date	new date
Date - *integer*	new date
Date1 - Date2	signed difference in days
Date += *integer*	new date
Date -= *integer*	new date
++Date	new date
Date++	old date
--Date	new date
Date--	old date

Note that in an expression such as `Date + `*integer*, the integer could have a negative value, in which case you are really subtracting, not adding.

You might be able to borrow ideas/code from the constructor problem that added support for yesterday, today, and tomorrow. In two of these cases, you had to add/subtract one day to/from a Date. This can be used as the building block for almost all the operators above.

Overloading [ ]

Because the `List` class contains an array of elements, we can define subscripting to access a specific element within that array, as follows:

```
    class List {
            int elem[3];
    public:
            List(int e0 = 0, int e1 = 0, int e2 = 0);
            void print(const char *name = "??") const;

            int &operator[](int i);
    };
```

```
#include <iostream.h>

main()
{
        List list1(3, 6, 0);

        list1.print("list1");
        list1[1] = 8;
        cout << "list1[1] = " << list1[1] << '\n';

        return 0;
}
int &List::operator[](int i)
{
        return elem[i];
}
```

The output produced is:

```
List list1 => [3:6:0]
list1[1] = 8
```

It is necessary to return the array element by reference in order to allow a subscripted expression to be used in the context of a modifiable lvalue, such as in the assignment above.

Neither C nor C++ provides array-bounds checking, and out-of-range subscripts can be difficult to find. However, because we are providing our own function to implement subscripting, we can take whatever action we want, including validating the incoming subscript. While this kind of error-checking is easy to perform, you need to consider what to do when an error is detected. Because you are in the middle of evaluating an expression, you might not want simply to complain and terminate the program. Instead, you might want to issue a message and return a valid value so the computation can continue.

When you use [] with arrays of built-in types, the compiler makes sure the offset has an integer type. However, the compiler does not do this checking when [] is overloaded. What happens is that list1[1.234] is treated as list1[1].

If we have an array of Lists, we can use [] twice: once to subscript the array and once to select an element within the resulting List. For example:

```
main()
{
        int val;

        List list1[] = {
                List(3, 6, 0),
                List(1, 2)
        };
```

```
                List list2[][2] = {
                        {List(1, 2, 3), List(4, 5, 6)},
                        {List(7, 8, 9)}
                };

                list1[1].print("list1[1]");
                val = list1[1][1];
                cout << "val = " << val << '\n';

                list2[0][1].print("list2[0][1]");
                val = list2[0][1][2];
                cout << "val = " << val << '\n';

                return 0;
        }
```

The output produced is:

```
List list1[1] => [1:2:0]
val = 2
List list2[0][1] => [4:5:6]
val = 6
```

In the case of `list1[1][1]`, the left `[]` has the usual meaning and selects an element within the array `list1`. The right `[]` causes the subscript operator function to be called. Similarly, in `list2[0][1][2]` the left two `[]` operators select an element in the 2-D array `list2`, while the right `[]` uses the operator function.

There are a number of differences between built-in subscripting and subscripting provided by overloaded functions. In the overloaded case, we have the following possibilities:

- By storing the array size inside the List, we can create a list whose size is not a compile-time constant.

- We could define a List so that its first element has a subscript other than zero, simply by adding or subtracting a value from each subscript passed into the overloaded operator function.

- The subscript need not be an integer expression. It could, for example, be a string.

- While built-in subscripting is commutative, this is not the case (and cannot be made the case) for overloaded versions. That is, `a[i]` is not equivalent to `i[a]`.

Overloading ( )

Overloading the function call operator ( ) is a little different, since in its usual role, it can have zero or more operands in a comma-separated argument list. When overloaded, this operator can continue to have a variable number of operands. In the following example, three different operator functions are defined for this operator. And you might expect, they are called on the basis of the argument list specified:

```
#include <iostream.h>

class List {
        int elem[3];
public:
        List(int e0 = 0, int e1 = 0, int e2 = 0);
        void print(const char *name = "??") const;

        void operator()(int i, int newvalue);
        void operator()(int start, int end, int newvalue);
        void operator()(int start, int end, int step, int newvalue);
};

main()
{
        List list1(3, 6, 0);

        list1.print("list1");
        list1(0, -2);             // set [0] to -2
        list1.print("list1");
        list1(1, 2, -5);          // set [1] and [2] to -5
        list1.print("list1");
        list1(0, 2, 2, -7);       // set [0] and [2] to -7
        list1.print("list1");

        return 0;
}

void List::operator()(int i, int newvalue)
{
        elem[i] = newvalue;
}

void List::operator()(int start, int end, int newvalue)
{
        for (int j = start; j <= end; ++j)
                elem[j] = newvalue;
}
```

```
void List::operator()(int start, int end, int step, int newvalue)
{
        for (int j = start; j <= end; j += step)
                elem[j] = newvalue;
}
```

The output produced is:

```
List list1 => [3:6:0]
List list1 => [-2:6:0]
List list1 => [-2:-5:-5]
List list1 => [-7:-5:-7]
```

The three functions all assign values to an existing List. The first version takes two arguments: the number of the element to be assigned and the value it should take on. The second version specifies a range of elements, and the third further adds a step.

The same effect can be achieved simply by using equivalent overloaded member functions:

```
void init(int i, int newvalue);
void init(int start, int end, int newvalue);
void init(int start, int end, int step, int newvalue);
```

Certainly this approach is more understandable, since the function name provides a clue to its purpose.

Class-Specific Versions of new and delete

The new and delete operators can be overloaded on a per-class basis. For example:

```
#include <iostream.h>
#include <stddef.h>

class List {
        int elem[3];
public:
        List(int e0 = 0, int e1 = 0, int e2 = 0);

        void * operator new(size_t size);
        void operator delete(void *pv, size_t size);
};

class Circle {
        long xorigin;
        long yorigin;
        unsigned long radius;
```

```
public:
        Circle(unsigned long rad = 1);
};

main()
{
/*1A*/  double *pd = new double;
/*2A*/  List *pl1 = new List;
/*3A*/  List *pl2 = new List[5];
/*4A*/  List *pl3 = ::new List;
/*5A*/  Circle *pcircle = new Circle;

// ...

/*1B*/  delete pd;
/*2B*/  delete pl1;
/*3B*/  delete [] pl2;
/*4B*/  ::delete pl3;
/*5B*/  delete pcircle;

        return 0;
}
void * List::operator new(size_t size)
{
        cout << size << " bytes requested of List::new\n";

        return 0;       // no memory is actually allocated
}
void List::operator delete(void *pv, size_t size)
{
        cout << "List::delete called with size " << size << '\n';
}
```

The output produced by one implementation is:

```
6 bytes requested of List::new
List::delete called with size 6
```

We have provided versions of **new** and **delete** only for the class **List**. However, these versions are used only for case 2A. The allocation of built-in types, such as in case 1A, is still done by the generic **new** and **delete** versions. And because arrays of any kind, including arrays of class objects, always use the generic versions too, case 3A does not use the overloaded versions, even though Lists are involved. In case 4A, we are allocating a List object, but we request to use the generic version of **new** instead by prefixing it with the scope resolution operator ::. And finally, case 5A involves the allocation of a Circle. Since there is no overloaded version for this class, the generic version is used instead.

The **new** operator must be overloaded by having one argument of type `size_t`. **delete** operator functions can have either one or two arguments. The first must be of type `void *`, and the second must be of type `size_t`. The **new** function must return a `void *`, and zero must be returned to indicate allocation failure. It must also return a distinct non-null pointer when given an argument of zero. The **delete** function must accept a zero argument with no ill side effects.

Overloading the I/O Operators << and >>

C++'s I/O can easily be extended to handle user-defined types. Until now, we have achieved class I/O via print member functions. We shall now see how the << and >> operators can be overloaded to achieve much the same result.

The operators << and >> already know how to handle all the built-in scalar types and null-terminated character arrays. (They cannot handle other array types or multidimensional arrays, structures, unions, or enumerations, however.) How do they do this? These basic types are handled by operator overload functions. For example, if you take a look inside the C++ standard header `iostream.h`, you will see something like the following:

```
class ostream {
// ...
public:
        ostream &operator<<(char);
        ostream &operator<<(int);
        ostream &operator<<(const char *);
        ostream &operator<<(double);
// ...
};

class istream {
// ...
public:
        istream &operator>>(char *);
        istream &operator>>(char &c);
        istream &operator>>(int &i);
        istream &operator>>(double &d);
// ...
};
```

The class `ostream` is used for standard output, which is where `cout` writes. The `istream` class is provided for `cin`. Each of these classes has an operator function for each of the scalar types as well as for `char` arrays.

For output, `char` values are treated differently than `int` is. That is, there is no automatic widening. In the case of `cout << c`, where `c` is a `char`, the character is displayed in its printed form. For `cout << i`, where `i` is an `int`, the value of the integer is displayed instead.

On input, there are two operator functions for handling characters. One expects a `char` by address, and that is used to read into an array of `char`. The other expects a `char` by reference, and that is used to read in a single `char`. This explains why you do not have to use the `&` operator in front of the character on input, as you do with `scanf`.

Let's overload `<<` and `>>` for a user-defined class:

```
#include <iostream.h>

class List {
        int elem[3];
public:
        List(int e0 = 0, int e1 = 0, int e2 = 0);

        friend istream &operator>>(istream &istr, List &l);
        friend ostream &operator<<(ostream &ostr, const List &l);
};
```

We need to make these operator functions friends, because their left operands are not an object of class `List`. The right operand is of the given class, however, for both input and output. Remember that the result produced by these operators can be used in some larger context, so we must pass it along via the `return`. When we use something such as:

```
cout << a << " " << b << "\n";
```

we are constructing an output set from individual components. Because these operators associate from left to right, the precedence is:

```
((((cout << a) << " ") << b) << "\n");
```

Therefore, the output from `a` is added to the output stream, and to that is added the output from `" "`, and so on, until all output has been concatenated into the `ostream`. Thus, the left operand to `<<` is `cout`'s stream `ostream` passed by reference, and this operator passes along this stream after having added the right operand to it. Similarly, all `>>` operator functions get an `istream` by reference as their left operand and must produce a result of the same type so it can be passed along:

```
main()
{
        int i, j;
        List list1;
```

```
        cin >> i >> list1 >> j;

        cout << "i = " << i << ", list1 = " << list1
             << ", j = " << j << '\n';

        return 0;
}
```

Given the input:

```
10 [100:20:546] 5
```

The output produced is:

```
i = 10, list1 = [100:20:546], j = 5
```

White space in the input is optional. For example, the same output is produced from all three of the following inputs:

```
10 [100:20:546] 5
10[100:20:546]5
10 [ 100 : 20 : 546 ] 5
```

The operator functions are:

```
istream &operator>>(istream &istr, List &l)
{
        char c;

// read in and ignore [, :, and ] characters

        istr >> c >> l.elem[0] >> c >> l.elem[1] >> c >> l.elem[2] >> c;

        return istr;
}
ostream &operator<<(ostream &ostr, const List &l)
{
        ostr << '[' << l.elem[0] << ':' << l.elem[1]
             << ':' << l.elem[2] << ']';

        return ostr;
}
```

Obviously, we could add code to validate the input, checking that the punctuation characters used are correct.

If we compare the output operator function with the `print` member function we have been using thus far, we see that the only real difference is that with the member function we could pass zero or more arguments, and we used this to pass in the object's name. With the operator function approach, the only arguments passed in are the two operands; we cannot pass anything extra.

We can overload the I/O operators to display the value of an enumerated type in a rational manner. For example:

```
#include <iostream.h>

enum color {red, green, white, blue, black, brown};
ostream &operator<<(ostream &ostr, enum color c);

main()
{
        color c1 = red;
        color c2 = blue;

        cout << "c1 is " << c1 << ", c2 is " << c2 << '\n';

        return 0;
}

ostream &operator<<(ostream &ostr, enum color c)
{
        static const char *names[] = {
                "red", "green", "white",
                "blue", "black", "brown"
        };

        ostr << names[c];

        return ostr;
}
```

The output produced is:

```
c1 is red, c2 is blue
```

Exercise 10

Define the << and >> operators for `Date` objects, for output and input, respectively. Ideally, the input function should be able to handle any valid date format. At a minimum, accept dates of the format mm/dd/yyyy, where years less than 100 are taken as being in the 20th century. Display dates as dd-Mmm-yyyy. Test the program using the date 09/08/1923.

What are the trade-offs compared with the `print` function version?

Assigning and Copying Class Objects

There are a number of contexts in which an object can be copied. They are:

- Assigning the value of one object to another.

- Passing an object by value to a function.

- Returning an object by value from a function.

- Initializing a new object by using an initializer.

The following code fragment contains an instance of each:

```
List list1(3, 6, 0);
List list2 = list1;      // initialize

list2 = f(list1);        // pass and return by value
list2 = list1;           // assign
```

Everything works just fine; when an object is copied, each of its members gets copied individually, resulting in a complete duplicate. However, what if the class is not self-contained? That is, what if it contains a pointer member that points outside the object? Making an identical copy of the object would make both copies point to the same thing. Let's see what happens when we try the same operations on Strings:

```
#include <iostream.h>
#include <string.h>

class String {
        unsigned length;
        char *ptext;
public:
        String(const char *pc = 0);
        ~String();
        void changestr(const char *pc);
        void print(const char *name = "??") const;
};

main()
{
        String s1("ab");

        s1.print("s1");

        String s2 = s1;
        s2.print("s2");

        s1.changestr("someothertext");
        s1.print("s1");
        s2.print("s2"); // ??

        return 0;
}
```

If you make a copy of a String, both string descriptors point to the same text. Then if you modify one of the Strings, the other String descriptor is no longer reliable. For example, the output produced from the example above is:

```
In constructor
String s1{2:"ab"}
String s2{2:"ab"}
In change
String s1{13:"someothertext"}
String s2{2:"???"}
In destructor
In destructor
```

When the String pointed to by s1 was changed (in terms of contents and length), s1 was updated correctly. However, s2 thinks it is still pointing at a two-character string. When **changestr** is called, it deletes the memory used to store the string previously pointed to, and it allocates new memory. Therefore, the address stored in s2 points to where the string used to be stored, not to where it is now. Therefore, s2 is unreliable, and it has the wrong length.

The rest of the program follows:

```
String::String(const char *pc)
{
        cout << "In constructor\n";
        if (pc == 0) {  // string is empty
                length = 0;
                ptext = 0;
        }
        else {
                length = strlen(pc);
                ptext = new char [length + 1];
                strcpy(ptext, pc);
        }
}


String::~String()
{
        cout << "In destructor\n";
        if (ptext != 0) {       // if string not empty delete it
                delete [] ptext;
        }
}

void String::print(const char *name) const
{
        cout << "String " << name << "{" << length << ":\""
             << (length != 0 ? ptext : "") << "\"}\n";
}

void String::changestr(const char *pc)
{
        cout << "In change\n";
        if (ptext != 0)         // delete old string if any
                delete [] ptext;

        if (pc == 0) {          // new string is null
                length = 0;
                ptext = 0;
        }
```

```
        else {
                length = strlen(pc);
                ptext = new char [length + 1];
                strcpy(ptext, pc);
        }
}
```

Clearly, simple assignment is insufficient for classes of this kind. Instead, what we need is to create a copy of the text for each String as well. We can solve part of the problem by using a special member function known as a *copy constructor*.

A copy constructor has the general form:

```
C::C(const C &)
```

where C is the class name. That is, it is a constructor that takes only one argument, which is of the class type, is passed by reference, and is `const`-qualified.

Once a copy constructor has been defined, the previous example produces the output:

```
In constructor
String s1{2:"ab"}
In copy constructor
String s2{2:"ab"}
In change
String s1{13:"someothertext"}
String s2{2:"ab"}
In destructor
In destructor
```

Notice that when s1 is copied to s2, s2's pointer points to a different place than does s1's. This is because the copy constructor made a copy of the text, and s2 points to that duplicate. Now when the first string is modified, the second is unaffected, as shown.

Here is the source for the copy constructor:

```
String::String(const String &s) // copy constructor
{
        cout << "In copy constructor\n";
        length = s.length;
        if (s.ptext == 0)
                ptext = 0;
        else {
                ptext = new char [length + 1];
                strcpy(ptext, s.ptext);
        }
}
```

Assigning and Copying Class Objects

The copy constructor approach correctly handles the case of objects in initializers and passing and returning objects by value. However, it does not completely handle the case of assignment between two existing objects. For example:

```
main()
{
        String s1("ab");
        String s2;

        s1.print("s1");
        s2 = s1;
        s2.print("s2");

        s1.changestr("someothertext");
        s1.print("s1");
        s2.print("s2");

        return 0;
}
```

The output produced is:

```
In constructor
In constructor
String s1{2:"ab"}
String s2{2:"ab"}
In change
String s1{13:"someothertext"}
String s2{2:"???"}
In destructor
In destructor
```

Once again, s2's length is wrong, and its pointer points to the location previously occupied by the string.

To solve the assignment case, we need to overload the assignment operator as well. The operator function is as follows:

```
String &String::operator=(const String &s)
{
        cout << "In operator=\n";
        if (this == &s)          // assigning a string to itself?
                return *this;

        if (ptext != 0)          // is there an old string?
                delete [] ptext;
```

```
            length = s.length;
            if (s.ptext == 0)        // is there a new string?
                    ptext = 0;
            else {
                    ptext = new char [length + 1];
                    strcpy(ptext, s.ptext);
            }

            return *this;
    }
```

With this addition, the program produces the following output:

```
In constructor
In constructor
String s1{2:"ab"}
In operator=
String s2{2:"ab"}
In change
String s1{13:"someothertext"}
String s2{2:"ab"}
In destructor
In destructor
```

Now assignment works correctly too.

Note that in the operator function, we first check to see if the object is being assigned to itself. If this is the case, we have no work to do. In fact, we must be careful not to delete the text to which the destination points, as that would also delete the text to which the source points.

Conversion Functions

It is possible to convert an expression of a given class type to another type, even another class type. You achieve this by what really amounts to overloading the functional notation version of the cast operator. This operator function actually is called whenever implicit conversion is needed. For example:

```
    #include <iostream.h>

    class Circle {
            long xorigin;
            long yorigin;
            unsigned long radius;
    public:
            Circle(long xo, long yo, unsigned long rad = 1);
            void print(const char *name = "??") const;
```

```
            operator int() { return radius; };   // inline version
            operator double();                    // non-inline
};


Circle::operator double(){
        return xorigin;
}
```

The `operator int` function converts a Circle to an `int`, while `operator double` converts a Circle to a `double`. In this example, neither of these claims to do anything useful; they simply demonstrate the syntax needed.

The code continues:

```
main()
{
        Circle c1(1, 2, 5);
        int i = c1;            // assign Circle to int
        double d = c1;         // assign Circle to double

        c1.print("c1");
        cout << "i = " << i << ", d = " << d << '\n';

        return 0;
}
```

The output produced is:

```
Circle c1 := (1:2:5)
i = 5, d = 1
```

Rules of Thumb

When overloading operators, keep the following things in mind:

- Use `const` on any explicitly declared incoming arguments passed by reference or address if the operator function has no business modifying them.

- Make the operator function a `const` function if the left operand should not be modified by that function.

- Watch out for code explosion when making operator functions `inline`.

- Choose your operators with care when overloading them. For example, making + mean subtraction is obviously silly, while defining ++ for a Circle has no intuitive meaning.

- You can implement many useful operations by using member functions instead of overloaded operators. For example, a member function called `invert` is more intuitive to use for a matrix class than is any of the operators. This is particularly true when you are thinking of overloading the function call operator.

- When an operator function returns an object, think carefully about whether it should be returned by value or by reference. To help decide which, you need to think of all the possible contexts in which the operator will be used.

Exercise 11

Once we start performing arithmetic operations on dates, dealing with them as separate day, month, and year members can get messy. If a date were stored as a year and Julian day, certain operations would be simpler, and if it were stored as a "super" Julian day that included the year as well, things might be simplified even more. Of course, certain other operations then would involve more work. For example, the constructor supplying day, month, and year would no longer be trivial; it would involve a Julian conversion. Similarly, the `print` function would need to convert from internal Julian format on each output, as would the I/O operators. Think of the ramifications of changing the way in which the date is represented. This problem is intended to be thought-provoking only; no solution is provided.

Part IV

Beyond Simple Classes

Chapter 11

Advanced Topics

In this book, I intentionally did not cover in depth a number of topics. They are templates, inheritance, and exception handling. Each of these topics is introduced briefly in this chapter.

Templates

Templates provide a generic way to implement a family of related functions and classes. For example, when a vector class is designed, it is tedious and error-prone to define an `int` version of that class completely separate from an `unsigned long` or `double` version. Essentially, the member sets of these classes, and the sources for their member functions, are identical; only the types of members, arguments, and return values change according to the vector type.

By allowing one generic class and member function set to be defined containing type placeholders, we can construct a vector of a specific type by using the corresponding template with a type parameter. In that sense, templates are similar to function-like macros.

The primary advantage of templates is that they ensure that all versions of a class or function set are identical, thereby guaranteeing consistency when the class and functions are initially defined and when they are modified.

Templates are implemented by the keyword `template`. A version of templates was introduced in AT&T's R3.0 and is partially or completely supported by a growing number of commercial implementations. Note, however, that the version to be adopted by Standard C++ has not yet been finalized.

Inheritance

Inheritance involves the use of *derived classes*. If class B contains all the members of class A as a subset, class B actually can share class A's members by *inheriting* them. We do this by defining class B to be derived from class A. For example, a point class contains the coordinates for a point, along with some member functions. A circle class could be derived from the point class, since a circle also needs a point as its origin.

When a class is derived from one other class only, we have what is called *single inheritance*. When a class is derived from more than one other class, we have *multiple inheritance*.

An important aspect of derived classes is the ability to have member functions by the same name at different levels of a class hierarchy. The implementation determines at run time which version of such functions to use. This involves the use of *virtual functions* and is referred to as *polymorphism*.

Inheritance is implemented by the keywords `protected` and `virtual` and by a new use of the colon punctuator in a class definition.

Exception Handling

The detection and treatment of errors is an important concern in class design. One example in particular is a failure during memory allocation. Another involves recovery from range errors in overloaded operator functions such as array-bounds checking for the [] operator.

The machinery provided in earlier releases of C++ is insufficient if a complete job is to be done. Therefore, a version of exception handling was introduced in AT&T's R3.0 and is partially or completely supported by a growing number of commercial implementations. Note, however, that the version to be adopted by Standard C++ has not yet been finalized.

Exception handling is implemented by the keywords `catch`, `throw`, and `try`.

Part V

Appendixes

Appendix A

Operator Precedence

Operator	Associativity
::	Right to Left
() [] -> . ++ --	Left to Right
! ~ ++ -- + - * & (*type*) sizeof new delete	Right to Left
.* ->*	Left to Right
* / %	Left to Right
+ -	Left to Right
<< >>	Left to Right
< <= > >=	Left to Right
== !=	Left to Right
&	Left to Right
^	Left to Right
|	Left to Right
&&	Left to Right
||	Left to Right
?:	Right to Left
= += -= *= /= %= >>= <<= &= ^= |=	Right to Left
,	Left to Right

The operator ( ) represents both function call and function-notation cast.

Postfix versions of ++ and -- have higher precedence than their prefix counterparts, just as in Standard C.

The rows of operators in the table are shown in decreasing order of precedence, from top to bottom. The ordering of operators in any given table row is arbitrary. Associativity applies to the order in which operators exist in a given expression, not in a row of the precedence table.

Appendix B

Keywords

C++ reserves the following source tokens as keywords:

asm[1,2]	continue	float	new[1]	signed	try[1,2]
auto	default	for	operator[1]	sizeof	typedef
break	delete[1]	friend[1]	private[1]	static	union
case	do	goto	protected[1,2]	struct	unsigned
catch[1,2]	double	if	public[1]	switch	virtual[1,2]
char	else	inline[1]	register	template[1,2]	void
class[1]	enum	int	return	this[1]	volatile
const	extern	long	short	throw[1,2]	while

---

[1] These keywords are specific to C++ and do not exist in C.
[2] These keywords are not discussed in this book.

Appendix C

Compatibility With Old Releases

With each release of C++, new features have been added, some have changed, and others have been removed. This appendix identifies these features to help you port code based on releases prior to R2.1.

1. In R2.0, the type qualifiers `const` and `volatile` were defined for member functions as well as data. When a member function is so qualified, the qualification applies to the object being operated on.

2. Prior to R2.1, in certain cases where arguments were passed to functions by reference, the compiler generated temporary objects. R2.1 considers these cases to be invalid. The old behavior is demonstrated by the following code:

   ```
   void f(int &i);

   void test()
   {
           char c = 'A';

   /*1*/   f(c);           // error in R2.1
   /*2*/   f(5);           // error in R2.1
   }

   void f(int &i)
   {
           i = 987;        // modify incoming int
   }
   ```

   In cases 1 and 2, we pass arguments that do not quite match what is expected. In such cases, the compiler was required to create a temporary object (of type `int` in this case), assign the actual argument's value to it, which resulted in the appropriate conversion, and then pass that temporary object by reference. Of course, changing i inside f has no real effect, since this results in the temporaries' being modified. And since these temporaries are created at each such call, they have no name and cannot be otherwise accessed. That is, they get changed, but their changed values can never be used.

A similar situation occurred in the following:

```
void test()
{
        int &ri = 123;          // error in R2.1
        double d = 1.23;
        int &rj = d;            // error in R2.1

        ri = 10;                // change copy of constant
        rj = 0;                 // change copy of d
}
```

3. Prior to R2.1, there was no way to distinguish between overloaded prefix and postfix versions of ++ and --.

4. Prior to R2.0, a keyword called **overload** was defined. Although this keyword no longer is part of C++, implementations may continue to recognize it as such for backward compatibility.

5. Prior to R2.1, the syntax for deleting an array was **delete** [*size*] **addr**, where *size* was required. With R2.1, the [] must be empty.

Appendix D

C and C++ Compatibility Issues

There are a number of issues you should consider when moving C code to a C++ environment:

1. Unlike C, C++ requires *all* characters in an identifier to be significant.

2. Identifiers containing two consecutive underscores are reserved for use by C++ implementations.

3. C++ has a number of keywords that might otherwise have been used as identifiers in C programs. They are asm, catch, class, delete, friend, inline, new, operator, private, protected, public, template, this, throw, try, and virtual. In addition, the obsolete C++ keyword overload may still be recognized as a keyword by some compilers.

4. In C, single-character character constants have type int. In C++, they have type char.

5. In C++, you cannot take the address of main or call it recursively.

6. Like C, C++ allows an enumerated type, or any enumeration constants defined for that type, to be used in an integer context. However, unlike C, C++ does not allow the reverse. That is, when an enumerated type is expected, an integer type will not be accepted as being compatible. Also, in C++, enumeration types are distinct and are not assignment-compatible with each other.

7. In C, enumeration constants have type int. In C++, they have the type of their parent enumeration type.

8. C++ does not permit types to be defined in a sizeof expression, a cast expression, or the return or argument type parts of a function declaration.

9. C permits you to jump into a block, using either switch or goto, thereby bypassing the initialization of local variables. C++ prohibits this.

10. In C, if you **return** without a value from a non-**void** function, the value actually returned is undefined. C++ requires that you return a value for such functions. This is an issue that particularly affects **main**, because many C programmers return from it without giving a specific return value, despite the fact that **main** is not a **void** function.

11. C++ does not support C's old-style function declarations or definitions.

12. In C++, the function declarations **void f()** and **void f(void)** are equivalent. In C, they are not, since the first is a function taking an unknown number of arguments.

13. In C, an undeclared identifier followed by a (token was taken as a call to a function that returned an **int**. In C++, every function call must be in the scope of a prototype; no defaults are applied.

14. In C, an object definition at file scope having the **const** qualifier but not the **static** storage class specifier causes that identifier to have external linkage. In C++, it has internal linkage unless it also contains the keyword **extern**.

15. Unlike C, C++ requires a **const**-qualified object definition to contain an explicit initializer.

16. When a structure or union type definition is nested inside another structure or union type, the inner type is visible at the outer level in C. In C++, the inner type is not visible outside that inner scope.

17. In C, the definition **char c[3] = "abc";** causes the array **c** to have no trailing null terminator; it is quietly discarded. In C++, this is an error because there is insufficient room in the array for the complete initializer, which includes the implicit trailing null character.

18. Unlike C, C++ requires an explicit cast when assigning a **void** pointer to a non-**void** data pointer. This most likely will be a problem when dealing with return values from **malloc**, **calloc**, **realloc**, and the **mem*** functions.

Appendix E

Solutions to Exercises

Exercise 1

Let's begin by isolating all the class-specific support in a header. We will refer to this header by the generic name `date.h`. However, for the sake of keeping each solution separate, the incremental versions of this header actually will be called `date01.h`, `date02.h`, `date03.h`, and so on, where each version corresponds to a different solution:

```
// ----------- date01.h -----------

typedef unsigned short year_t;
typedef unsigned char month_t;
typedef unsigned char day_t;

typedef unsigned int display_t;
```

The day, month, and year variables can be stored as various types. In the case of day and month, we could choose any of the eight signed and unsigned integer types. In the case of year, all except **signed char** and **unsigned char** will suffice. To allow the solution to be implemented efficiently in terms of space and/or speed, we will use **typedef** names. That way, the mapping of the variables can be changed to accommodate various architectures, such as word machines. These members' values will start at 1, not 0.

The need for the `display_t` type will be seen later. The class definition continues:

```
class Date {
        year_t year;
        month_t month;
        day_t day;
```

```
#ifdef VALIDATE_DATE
        void validate_date();
#endif
```

The private members include `year`, `month`, and `day`, and a function to validate the contents of a date object. Here are the public members:

```
public:
        static const char *MonthNamesAbbrev[13];
        static const day_t DaysInMonth[2][13];

        void init(year_t yy, month_t mm, day_t dd);
        void print(const char *object_name) const;
};
```

The public members include two `static` data members and two public functions. The two arrays contain the number of days in each month, in both a leap and a non-leap year, and the abbreviated month names. They are `static`, so they are shared by all `Date` objects and exist even if there are no `Date` objects. Each array has 13 elements, with the first being wasted to allow the more natural 1-based indexing.

Because `print` has no business modifying its incoming argument, the prototype contains `const`. Similarly, it has no business modifying the `Date` object it is printing, so the function is `const`-qualified. This allows it to work for both `const`- and non-`const`-qualified objects but not on `volatile`-qualified objects. The argument to `print` is not really necessary but can be useful.

The header continues:

```
int isleapyear(year_t yy);

#ifdef VALIDATE_DATE
        #define YEAR_MIN        1800
        #define YEAR_MAX        2100
#else
        #define validate_date() ((void)0)
#endif

#define YEAR_DEFAULT    1800
#define MONTH_DEFAULT   1
#define DAY_DEFAULT     1

// ----------- date01.h -----------
```

The function `isleapyear` does as its name suggests: tests if a given year is a leap year. (It could have been defined inside the class.)

If the macro **VALIDATE_DATE** is defined when this header is included, several validation macros are defined. If validation is not selected, all calls to the function `validate_date` get turned into void expressions and so are effectively removed.

The *_DEFAULT macros are used as default values as appropriate, such as in recovering from invalid input dates.

Here is the main program:

```
// ----------- lab01.cpp -----------

#include <iostream.h>
#include <iomanip.h>

#define VALIDATE_DATE
#include "date01.h"

const char *Date::MonthNamesAbbrev[] = {
        "", "Jan", "Feb", "Mar", "Apr", "May", "Jun",
            "Jul", "Aug", "Sep", "Oct", "Nov", "Dec"
};

const day_t Date::DaysInMonth[][13] = {
        {0, 31, 28, 31, 30, 31, 30, 31, 31, 30, 31, 30, 31},
        {0, 31, 29, 31, 30, 31, 30, 31, 31, 30, 31, 30, 31}  // leap
};

Date date1;
static Date date2;

main()
{
        Date date3;

        date1.init(1993,  5, 10);
        date1.print("date1");

        date2.init(  56, 10,  5);
        date2.print("date2");

        date3.init(  -5,2.5,260);        // all are invalid
        date3.print("date3");

        return 0;
}
```

```
void Date::init(year_t yy, month_t mm, day_t dd)
{
        if (yy >= 0 && yy < 100)
                year = yy + 1900;
        else
                year = yy;

        day = dd;
        month = mm;

        validate_date();
}
```

The date is not validated until all of its parts have been stored in the Date object. From a certain perspective, this is too late. Specifically, when init is called in main, any arithmetic arguments will be converted—as if by casts—to the types in the prototype. This could result in truncation of larger integers or floating-point values or in conversion of negative values to unsigned equivalents or vice versa. That is, once init gets control, it may have lost the original argument values that were used in the call. The only way to be sure is to validate the arguments at their source.

Because the members year, month, and day could have unsigned integer types, we must be sure to avoid comparing them with negative values. Also, we must avoid expressions of the form day < 0 or day <= 0.

```
void Date::print(const char *object_name) const
{
        cout << "Date " << (object_name == 0 ? "??" : object_name)
             << " is " << setw(2) << setfill('0') << (display_t)day
             << "-" << MonthNamesAbbrev[month]
             << "-" << year << '\n';
}
```

Note the use of the (display_t) cast. Because we are allowing day to have any integer type, we must handle correctly its being a signed or unsigned char. In these cases, the compiler would output its value as a character, not as an integer. And on an ASCII machine, days in the range 1 through 31 result in a nonprintable character being output. The same would also apply to month. The cast is not necessary with year, since year has to be at least a short int to handle the required range. As such, the short would be promoted to int, and signed and unsigned int and long types would be output correctly.

It is very likely that day and month would really have the same underlying type. By making display_t have the widened version of that type, we can avoid this display problem.

The code continues:

```
#ifdef VALIDATE_DATE
void Date::validate_date()
{
        if (year < YEAR_MIN || year > YEAR_MAX) {
                cerr << "Year " << year << " is invalid\n";
                year = YEAR_DEFAULT;
        }

        if (month < 1 || month > 12) {
                cerr << "Month " << (display_t)month
                     << " is invalid\n";
                month = MONTH_DEFAULT;
        }

        if (day < 1 || day > DaysInMonth[isleapyear(year)][month]) {
                cerr << "Day " << (display_t)day
                     << " is invalid for month " << (display_t) month
                     << " in year " << year << '\n';
                day = DAY_DEFAULT;
        }
}
#endif

int isleapyear(year_t yy)          // expects yy > 99
{
        return (((yy & 3) == 0 && yy % 100 != 0) || yy % 400 == 0);
}

// ----------- lab01.cpp -----------
```

The output produced for the dates (1993, 5, 10), (56, 10, 5), and (−5, 2.5, 260) is:

```
Date date1 is 10-May-1993
Date date2 is 05-Oct-1956
Year 65531 is invalid
Date date3 is 04-Feb-1800
```

Remember that in this example, all private members had unsigned types. Thus, a year of −5 cast to **unsigned short** on a 16-bit, two's-complement machine results in a value of 65531. The **double** month value 2.5 is simply truncated and looks like the second month, February. The day value 260 is truncated and converted to an **unsigned char** resulting in a day of 4, which *is* in range.

The output produced for the invalid date only when the members were made **signed short**, **signed char**, and **signed char**, respectively, was:

```
Year -5 is invalid
Date date3 is 04-Feb-1800
```

The output produced when the members were all **signed int** or all **signed long int** was:

```
Year -5 is invalid
Day 260 is invalid for month 2 in year 1800
Date date3 is 01-Feb-1800
```

The output produced when the members were all **unsigned int** was:

```
Year 65531 is invalid
Day 260 is invalid for month 2 in year 1800
Date date3 is 01-Feb-1800
```

The output produced when the members were all **unsigned long int** was:

```
Year 4294967291 is invalid
Day 260 is invalid for month 2 in year 1800
Date date3 is 01-Feb-1800
```

Exercise 2

The additions and changes to `date.h` are quite straightforward:

```
// ----------- date02.h -----------

...
typedef unsigned short julian_t;

class Date {
        ...
public:
        ...
        void init(year_t yy, month_t mm, day_t dd);
        void init(const char *date_string);
        void init(year_t yy, julian_t julian);
        void init();
};
...
void jultomd(julian_t julian, year_t yy, month_t *mm, day_t *dd);

// ----------- date02.h -----------
```

The function `jultomd` converts a Julian day for a given year to the corresponding month and day. It is not a member function, although it could just as easily have been.

Exercise 2

The code follows. Functions that are unchanged from previous solutions are not duplicated here:

```cpp
// ----------- lab02.cpp -----------

#define VALIDATE_DATE

#include <iostream.h>
#include <iomanip.h>
#include <string.h>
#include <stdlib.h>
#include <ctype.h>

#include "date02.h"

Date date1;

main()
{
        date1.init(1993, 5, 10);
        date1.print("date1");

        date1.init("02-Mar-1990");
        date1.print("date1");

        date1.init("02-Mar-90");          // string too short
        date1.print("date1");

        date1.init("02/Mar/1990");        // '/'s instead of '-'s
        date1.print("date1");

        date1.init("02-Mar-yyyy");        // invalid year
        date1.print("date1");

        date1.init("02-MAR-1990");        // invalid month
        date1.print("date1");

        date1.init("dd-Mar-1990");        // invalid day
        date1.print("date1");

        date1.init(92, 61);               // March 1st - leap year
        date1.print("date1");

        date1.init(192, 400);             // invalid year and julian day
        date1.print("date1");
```

```
                date1.init();
                date1.print("date1");

                return 0;
        }


        void Date::init(const char *date_string) // expects "dd-Mmm-yyyy" or 0
        {
                year = YEAR_DEFAULT;
                month = MONTH_DEFAULT;
                day = DAY_DEFAULT;

                if (date_string == 0) {
                        return;
                }

#ifdef VALIDATE_DATE
                if (strlen(date_string) != 11) {
                        cerr << "Date \"" << date_string
                                << "\" incorrect length" << '\n';
                        return;
                }

                if (date_string[2] != '-' || date_string[6] != '-') {
                        cerr << "Date \"" << date_string
                                << "\" incorrect format" << '\n';
                        return;
                }

                if (!isdigit(date_string[0]) || !isdigit(date_string[1])) {
                        cerr << "Date \"" << date_string
                                << "\" has an invalid day" << '\n';
                }
                else
#endif
                        day = (day_t)atoi(&date_string[0]);
```

The explicit cast to **day_t** is unnecessary, since assigning to **day** would do the same conversion anyway. The explicit or implicit conversion could result in a problem for a negative day being converted to an unsigned type. However, a negative day would be trapped by the `isdigit` validation code above, because a minus sign is not a digit.

```
                int i;

                for (i = 1; i <= 12; ++i) {
                        if (strncmp(&date_string[3], MonthNamesAbbrev[i], 3)
                            == 0) {
                                month = i + 1;
                                goto found;
                        }
                }
#ifdef VALIDATE_DATE
        cerr << "Date \"" << date_string
                << "\" has an invalid month" << '\n';
#endif

        found:

#ifdef VALIDATE_DATE
        if (!isdigit(date_string[7]) || !isdigit(date_string[8]) ||
            !isdigit(date_string[9]) || !isdigit(date_string[10])) {
                cerr << "Date \"" << date_string
                        << "\" has an invalid year" << '\n';
        }
        else
#endif
                year = (year_t)atoi(&date_string[7]);

        validate_date();
}
```

As discussed above with the date conversion using `atoi`, the explicit cast to `year_t` is unnecessary here, too, for the same reasons.

```
void Date::init(year_t yy, julian_t julian)
{
        if (yy >= 0 && yy < 100) {
                year = yy + 1900;
        }
        else {
                year = yy;
        }

        jultomd(julian, year, &month, &day);

        validate_date();
}
```

```
void Date::init()
{
        year = YEAR_DEFAULT;
        month = MONTH_DEFAULT;
        day = DAY_DEFAULT;
}

void jultomd(julian_t julian, year_t yy, month_t *mm, day_t *dd)
{
        int i = isleapyear(yy);
        int j;

#ifdef VALIDATE_DATE
        if (julian < 1 || julian > (i ? 366 : 365)) {
                cerr << "Julian day " << (display_t)julian
                     << " is out of range\n";
                *mm = MONTH_DEFAULT;
                *dd = DAY_DEFAULT;
                return;
        }
#endif
```

The (display_t) cast is unnecessary, because the range of values for a Julian day requires at least a signed or unsigned short int type. As such, cerr would not output Julian as a character:

```
        *mm = 1;
        for (j = 1; j <= 12; ++j) {
                if (julian <= Date::DaysInMonth[i][j]) {
                        *dd = julian;
                        return;
                }
                else {
                        ++*mm;
                        julian -= Date::DaysInMonth[i][j];
                }
        }
```

Because this function is not a member of class Date, the Date:: selector is needed to access the static member arrays:

```
        /* won't get here unless julian out-of-range and VALIDATE_DATE off */
        *mm = MONTH_DEFAULT;
        *dd = DAY_DEFAULT;
}
```

```
// ----------- lab02.cpp -----------
```

The output produced is:

```
Date date1 is 10-May-1993
Date date1 is 02-Mar-1990
Date "02-Mar-90" incorrect length
Date date1 is 01-Jan-1800
Date "02/Mar/1990" incorrect format
Date date1 is 01-Jan-1800
Date "02-Mar-yyyy" has an invalid year
Date date1 is 02-Mar-1800
Date "02-MAR-1990" has an invalid month
Date date1 is 02-Jan-1990
Date "dd-Mar-1990" has an invalid day
Date date1 is 01-Mar-1990
Date date1 is 01-Mar-1992
Julian day 400 is out of range
Year 192 is invalid
Date date1 is 01-Jan-1800
Date date1 is 01-Jan-1800
```

Exercise 3

The additions and changes to **date.h** are as follows:

```
// ----------- date03.h -----------

...
class Date {
        ...
public:
        ...
        enum prtfmt {dd_Mmm_yyyy, dd_mm_yyyy, mm_dd_yyyy,
                yyyy_mm_dd, yyyy_jul};
        ...
        void print(const char *object_name= "??",
                enum prtfmt=dd_Mmm_yyyy) const;
};
...
year_t mdtojul(year_t yy, month_t mm, day_t dd);
...

// ----------- date03.h -----------
```

The enumeration constants could have been macros. However, by defining them as shown, they are public members of the `Date` class. To use them outside that class, you need the `Date::` selector. If they were macros, they would take up identifier namespace universally, not just within one class. Using that namespace pollution argument, you can argue a case that some of the macros (such as *_DEFAULT) perhaps also should be enumeration constants.

The main program follows:

```
// ----------- lab03.cpp -----------

#define VALIDATE_PRINT_FORMAT

#include <iostream.h>
#include <iomanip.h>

#include "date03.h"

Date date1;

main()
{
        date1.init(93, 3, 2);

        date1.print("date1", Date::dd_Mmm_yyyy);
        date1.print("date1", Date::dd_mm_yyyy);
        date1.print("date1", Date::mm_dd_yyyy);
        date1.print("date1", Date::yyyy_mm_dd);
        date1.print("date1", Date::yyyy_jul);
        date1.print("date1");           // default format
        date1.print();                  // default name and format

        return 0;
}
```

As `main` is not a member function of class `Date`, the `Date::` selectors are needed on all references to the print format enumeration constants:

```
void Date::print(const char *object_name,
        enum prtfmt print_format) const
{
        cout << "Date " << object_name << " is ";

        switch (print_format) {
```

Exercise 3

```
        case dd_Mmm_yyyy:

                cout << setw(2) << setfill('0') << (display_t)day
                    << "-" << MonthNamesAbbrev[month]
                    << "-" << year << '\n';

                break;

        case dd_mm_yyyy:

                cout << setw(2) << setfill('0') << (display_t)day
                    << "/" << setw(2) << (display_t)month
                    << "/" << year << '\n';

                break;

        case mm_dd_yyyy:

                cout << setw(2) << setfill('0') << (display_t)month
                    << "/" << setw(2) << (display_t)day
                    << "/" << year << '\n';

                break;

        case yyyy_mm_dd:

                cout << year
                    << "/" << setw(2) << setfill('0') << (display_t)month
                    << "/" << setw(2) << (display_t)day << '\n';

                break;

        case yyyy_jul:

                cout << year << ":" << setw(3) << setfill('0')
                    << (display_t)mdtojul(year, month, day) << '\n';

                break;
        }
}
```

```
year_t mdtojul(year_t yy, month_t mm, day_t dd)
{
        int i = isleapyear(yy);
        int j;
        year_t julian = 0;

        for (j = 1; j < mm; ++j) {
                julian += Date::DaysInMonth[i][j];
        }

        julian += dd;
        return julian;
}

// ----------- lab03.cpp -----------
```

The output produced is:

```
Date date1 is 02-Mar-1993
Date date1 is 02/03/1993
Date date1 is 03/02/1993
Date date1 is 1993/03/02
Date date1 is 1993:061
Date date1 is 02-Mar-1993
Date ?? is 02-Mar-1993
```

Exercise 4

The header contains the following changes:

```
// ----------- date04.h -----------

...
class Date {
        ...
        static const char *MonthNamesAbbrev[13];
        static const day_t DaysInMonth[2][13];

        day_t   GetDay() const           { return day; };
        month_t GetMonth() const         { return month; };
        year_t  GetYear() const          { return year; };

        void    SetDay(day_t dd)         { day = dd; };
        void    SetMonth(month_t mm)     { month = mm; };
        void    SetYear(year_t yy)       { year = yy; };
```

Exercise 4

The month name and day arrays are now accessed indirectly, via two new public member functions. Therefore, these arrays can now be private instead of public. This does not prohibit a public or private member function from accessing them directly. It does, however, prohibit direct access from nonmember functions. Similarly, the Set* and Get* data access member functions are also private.

The Set* and Get* functions are trivial, given the way in which a date is actually stored. Thus, it makes sense to have them be inline functions, so calling them is just like doing the underlying assignments, only we use functional notation to achieve it:

```
public:
        ...
        static const char *GetMonthNamesAbbrev(month_t mm) {
                return MonthNamesAbbrev[mm];
        }

        static day_t GetDaysInMonth(int leapflag, month_t mm) {
                return DaysInMonth[leapflag][mm];
        }
        ...
};
...

// ----------- date04.h -----------
```

Similarly, we can access the now-private month arrays via two trivial inline public static functions.

The changes to the code are many, and we must replace every direct access to the year, month, and day members and the month arrays:

```
// ----------- lab04.cpp -----------

#include <iostream.h>
#include <iomanip.h>
#include <string.h>
#include <stdlib.h>
#include <ctype.h>

#include "date04.h"

Date date1;

main()
{
        date1.init(1993, 5, 10);
        date1.print("date1");
```

```
        date1.init("02-Mar-1990");
        date1.print("date1");

        date1.init();
        date1.print("date1");

        date1.init(93, 3, 2);
        date1.print("date1", Date::dd_Mmm_yyyy);
        date1.print("date1", Date::yyyy_jul);

        return 0;
}

void Date::init(year_t yy, month_t mm, day_t dd)
{
        if (yy >= 0 && yy < 100) {
                SetYear(yy + 1900);
        }
        else {
                SetYear(yy);
        }

        SetDay(dd);
        SetMonth(mm);

        validate_date();
}

void Date::init(const char *date_string)  // expects "dd-Mmm-yyyy" or 0
{
        SetYear(YEAR_DEFAULT);
        SetMonth(MONTH_DEFAULT);
        SetDay(DAY_DEFAULT);

        if (date_string == 0) {
                return;
        }

#ifdef VALIDATE_DATE
        if (strlen(date_string) != 11) {
                cerr << "Date \"" << date_string
                     << "\" incorrect length" << '\n';
                return;
        }
```

```
                if (date_string[2] != '-' || date_string[6] != '-') {
                        cerr << "Date \"" << date_string
                             << "\" incorrect format" << '\n';
                        return;
                }

                if (!isdigit(date_string[0]) || !isdigit(date_string[1])) {
                        cerr << "Date \"" << date_string
                             << "\" has an invalid day" << '\n';
                }
                else
#endif
                        SetDay((day_t)atoi(&date_string[0]));


        int mon;

        for (mon = 1; mon <= 12; ++mon) {
                if (strncmp(&date_string[3],
                    GetMonthNamesAbbrev(mon), 3) == 0) {
                        SetMonth(mon);
                        goto found;
                }
        }

#ifdef VALIDATE_DATE
        cerr << "Date \"" << date_string
             << "\" has an invalid month" << '\n';
#endif

found:

#ifdef VALIDATE_DATE
        if (!isdigit(date_string[7]) || !isdigit(date_string[8]) ||
            !isdigit(date_string[9]) || !isdigit(date_string[10])) {
                cerr << "Date \"" << date_string
                     << "\" has an invalid year" << '\n';
        }
        else
#endif
                SetYear((year_t)atoi(&date_string[7]));

        validate_date();
}
```

```
void Date::init(year_t yy, julian_t julian)
{
        if (yy >= 0 && yy < 100) {
                SetYear(yy + 1900);
        }
        else {
                SetYear(yy);
        }

        day_t dd;
        month_t mm;

        jultomd(julian, GetYear(), &mm, &dd);
        SetMonth(mm);
        SetDay(dd);

        validate_date();
}

void Date::init()
{
        SetYear(YEAR_DEFAULT);
        SetMonth(MONTH_DEFAULT);
        SetDay(DAY_DEFAULT);
}

void Date::print(const char *object_name,
        enum prtfmt print_format) const
{
        cout << "Date " << object_name << " is ";

        switch (print_format) {

case dd_Mmm_yyyy:

        cout << setw(2) << setfill('0') << (display_t)GetDay()
            << "-" << GetMonthNamesAbbrev(GetMonth()) << "-"
            << GetYear() << '\n';
        break;

case dd_mm_yyyy:

        cout << setw(2) << setfill('0') << (display_t)GetDay()
            << "/" << setw(2) << (display_t)GetMonth() << "/"
            << GetYear() << '\n';
        break;
```

Exercise 4

```
    case mm_dd_yyyy:

            cout << setw(2) << setfill('0') << (display_t)GetMonth()
                 << "/" << setw(2) << (display_t)GetDay() << "/"
                 << GetYear() << '\n';
            break;


    case yyyy_mm_dd:

            cout << GetYear() << "/" << setw(2) << setfill('0')
                 << (display_t)GetMonth() << "/" << setw(2)
                 << (display_t)GetDay() << '\n';
            break;


    case yyyy_jul:

            cout << GetYear() << ":" << setw(3) << setfill('0')
                 << (display_t)mdtojul(GetYear(), GetMonth(), GetDay())
                 << '\n';
            break;
    }
}


year_t mdtojul(year_t yy, month_t mm, day_t dd)
{
        int leapflag = isleapyear(yy);
        int mon;
        year_t julian = 0;

        for (mon = 1; mon < mm; ++mon) {
                julian += Date::GetDaysInMonth(leapflag, mon);
        }

        julian += dd;
        return julian;
}


void jultomd(julian_t julian, year_t yy, month_t *mm, day_t *dd)
{
        int leapflag = isleapyear(yy);
        int mon;
```

```
#ifdef VALIDATE_DATE
        if (julian < 1 || julian > (leapflag ? 366 : 365)) {
                cerr << "Julian day " << (display_t)julian
                     << " is out of range\n";
                *mm = MONTH_DEFAULT;
                *dd = DAY_DEFAULT;
                return;
        }
#endif


        *mm = 1;
        for (mon = 1; mon <= 12; ++mon) {
                if (julian <= Date::GetDaysInMonth(leapflag, mon)) {
                        *dd = julian;
                        return;
                }
                else {
                        ++*mm;
                        julian -= Date::GetDaysInMonth(leapflag, mon);
                }
        }


/* won't get here unless julian out-of-range and VALIDATE_DATE off */
        *mm = MONTH_DEFAULT;
        *dd = DAY_DEFAULT;
}



#ifdef VALIDATE_DATE
void Date::validate_date()
{
        if (GetYear() < YEAR_MIN || GetYear() > YEAR_MAX) {
                cerr << "Year " << GetYear() << " is invalid\n";
                SetYear(YEAR_DEFAULT);
        }


        if (GetMonth() < 1 || GetMonth() > 12) {
                cerr << "Month " << (display_t)GetMonth()
                     << " is invalid\n";
                SetMonth(MONTH_DEFAULT);
        }
```

```
                    if (GetDay() < 1 || GetDay() >
                        GetDaysInMonth(isleapyear(GetYear()), GetMonth())) {
                            cerr << "Day " << (display_t)GetDay()
                                 << " is invalid for month "
                                 << (display_t) GetMonth()
                                 << " in year " << GetYear() << '\n';
                            SetDay(DAY_DEFAULT);
                    }
        }
        #endif

        // ----------- lab04.cpp -----------
```

The output produced is:

```
Date date1 is 10-May-1993
Date date1 is 02-Mar-1990
Date date1 is 01-Jan-1800
Date date1 is 02-Mar-1993
Date date1 is 1993:061
```

Exercise 5

The changes to the header are quite straightforward:

```
        // ----------- date05.h -----------

        ...
        class Date {
                ...
                void     GetToday();

        public:
                enum relday {yesterday, today, tomorrow};

                Date(year_t yy, month_t mm, day_t dd);
                Date(const char *date_string);
                Date(year_t yy, julian_t julian);
                Date(relday ytt);
                Date();
                ...
        };
        ...
        // ----------- date05.h -----------
```

We have a new private member function, GetToday, to get today's date. The four versions of the init function are renamed as corresponding constructors. A new constructor is declared that accepts one argument that is any one of the three new enumeration constants yesterday, today, and tomorrow.

Here is the main program:

```
// ----------- lab05.cpp -----------

#include <iostream.h>
#include <iomanip.h>
#include <time.h>

#include "date05.h"

main()
{
        Date date1[][2] = {
                {Date(Date::yesterday)},
                {Date(Date::today)},
                {Date(Date::tomorrow)}
        };

        int i, j;

        for (j = 0; j < 2; ++j) {
                for (i = 0; i < 3; ++i) {
                        cout << "date1[" << i << "][" << j << "] ";
                        date1[i][j].print("");
                }
        }

        return 0;
}
```

Because the initializer for each row is incomplete, unspecified trailing elements will be initialized by the default constructor.

The code continues:

```
Date::Date(enum relday ytt)
{
        day_t dd;
        month_t mm;
        year_t yy;
        int leapflag;
```

Exercise 5

```
                GetToday();
                switch (ytt) {
        case yesterday:
                dd = GetDay();
                mm = GetMonth();
                yy = GetYear();
                leapflag = isleapyear(yy);

                if (--dd >= 1) {                               // Month change?
                        SetDay(dd);                            // no
                }
                else {                                         // yes
                        SetDay(GetDaysInMonth(leapflag, mm == 1 ? 12 : mm - 1));
                        if (--mm >= 1) {                       // Year change?
                                SetMonth(mm);                  // no
                        }
                        else {                                 // yes
                                SetMonth(12);
                                SetYear(yy - 1);
                        }
                }
                break;

        case tomorrow:
                dd = GetDay();
                mm = GetMonth();
                yy = GetYear();
                leapflag = isleapyear(yy);

                if (++dd <= GetDaysInMonth(leapflag, mm)) {// Month change?
                        SetDay(dd);                            // no
                }
                else {                                         // yes
                        SetDay(1);
                        if (++mm <= 12) {                      // Year change?
                                SetMonth(mm);                  // no
                        }
                        else {                                 // yes
                                SetMonth(1);
                                SetYear(yy + 1);
                        }
                }
                break;
```

```
case today:
      break;

     }
}

void Date::GetToday()
{
     time_t t;
     struct tm *ptime;

     time(&t);                    // get calendar time
     ptime = localtime(&t);       // convert to local time

     SetDay(ptime->tm_mday);
     SetMonth(ptime->tm_mon + 1);
     SetYear(ptime->tm_year + 1900);
}

// ----------- lab05.cpp -----------
```

When the program was run on 01-Feb-1992, the output produced was as follows:

```
date1[0][0] Date   is 31-Jan-1992
date1[1][0] Date   is 01-Feb-1992
date1[2][0] Date   is 02-Feb-1992
date1[0][1] Date   is 01-Jan-1800
date1[1][1] Date   is 01-Jan-1800
date1[2][1] Date   is 01-Jan-1800
```

Exercise 6

The header is unchanged, and there are only two changes needed to the program, both in the constructor function:

```
// ----------- lab06.cpp -----------

#include <iostream.h>
#include <strstream.h>
#include <iomanip.h>
#include <string.h>
#include <ctype.h>
#include <time.h>
#include "date06.h"
```

```
main()
{
        Date date1("02-Mar-1990");
        date1.print("date1", Date::yyyy_mm_dd);

        Date date2("23-Nov-1982");
        date2.print("date2", Date::yyyy_mm_dd);

        return 0;
}
```

In the previous version of the constructor, we could pass the result produced by `atoi` into the `Set` function, as follows:

```
SetDay((day_t)atoi(&date_string[0]));
SetYear((year_t)atoi(&date_string[7]));
```

However, the syntax of the in-memory decoding operation requires that we decode directly into an object. We are now accessing the data members indirectly through the `Get*` and `Set*` functions, so we cannot decode into them directly. Instead, we need to create some temporaries, decode into them, and then use them to set the members, as follows:

```
int dd;            // Don't make type day_t

istrstream(&date_string[0], 2) >> dd;    // *** new
SetDay(dd);

...

year_t yy;

istrstream(&date_string[7], 4) >> yy;    // *** new
SetYear(yy);

// ---------- lab06.cpp ----------
```

Note that while it might seem intuitive to make `dd`'s type `day_t`, doing so can cause a real problem. Remember the need for the `display_t` type cited earlier? Well, a similar problem can occur here. The compiler looks at the type of `dd` to determine how to inspect the data being decoded, and if `dd` has some `char` type it will decode characters, not integers. As such, an ASCII character 1 will be decoded as 49 rather than as 1. Again, the problem should not exist for `yy`, since that cannot legitimately be a character type.

Given the input in `main`, the output is:

```
Date date1 is 1990/03/02
Date date2 is 1982/11/23
```

Exercise 7

The header has been augmented by three new public member functions:

```
// ----------- date07.h -----------

...
class Date {
        ...
public:
        ...
        Date MinDate(const Date &date2) const
        {
                return(CompareDate(date2) <= 0 ? *this : date2);
        }

        Date MaxDate(const Date &date2) const
        {
                return(CompareDate(date2) > 0 ? *this : date2);
        }

        int CompareDate(const Date &date2) const;
};
...

// ----------- date07.h -----------
```

As **MinDate** and **MaxDate** need to do almost the same thing, it seems reasonable to invent a third function **CompareDate** that compares dates and behaves much like **strcmp** and **memcmp**. (This function will also come in handy when we overload the comparison operators.) **MinDate** and **MaxDate** are trivial, so they are inlined. Note the presence of **const** to protect both date objects from being modified. The hidden argument **this** is passed by address, while the explicit argument is passed by reference.

The main program follows:

```
// ----------- lab07.cpp -----------

#include <iostream.h>
#include <iomanip.h>

#include "date07.h"
```

Exercise 7

```
main()
{
        Date date1(90, 5, 6);
        Date date2(90, 5, 6);
        Date date3(92, 1, 2);
        Date date4;

        date4 = date1.MaxDate(date3);
        date4.print("date4");

        date4 = date1.MinDate(date3);
        date4.print("date4");

        cout << "1/2 " << date1.CompareDate(date2) << '\n';
        cout << "1/3 " << date1.CompareDate(date3) << '\n';
        cout << "3/1 " << date3.CompareDate(date1) << '\n';

        return 0;
}

int Date::CompareDate(const Date &date2) const
{
        if (GetYear() < date2.GetYear()) {
                return -1;                      // date1 < date2
        }

        else if (GetYear() > date2.GetYear()) {
                return 1;                       // date1 > date2
        }

        else if (GetMonth() < date2.GetMonth()) {
                return -1;                      // date1 < date2
        }

        else if (GetMonth() > date2.GetMonth()) {
                return 1;                       // date1 > date2
        }

        else if (GetDay() < date2.GetDay()) {
                return -1;                      // date1 < date2
        }

        else if (GetDay() > date2.GetDay()) {
                return 1;                       // date1 > date2
        }
```

```
                else {
                        return 0;                       // date1 == date2
                }
        }
}

// ----------- lab07.cpp -----------
```

The output produced is:

```
Date date4 is 02-Jan-1992
Date date4 is 06-May-1990
1/2 0
1/3 -1
3/1 1
```

Exercise 8

The header is changed by adding the operator functions. Since they all rely on CompareDate to do the work, they are trivial and thus are inline:

```
        // ----------- date08.h -----------

        ...
        class Date {
                ...
        public:
                ...

// operators
                int operator==(const Date &date2) const   // Date1 == Date2
                {
                        return CompareDate(date2) == 0;
                }

                int operator!=(const Date &date2) const   // Date1 != Date2
                {
                        return CompareDate(date2) != 0;
                }

                int operator>(const Date &date2) const    // Date1 > Date2
                {
                        return CompareDate(date2) > 0;
                }
```

```
                int operator>=(const Date &date2) const    // Date1 >= Date2
                {
                        return CompareDate(date2) >= 0;
                }

                int operator<(const Date &date2) const     // Date1 < Date2
                {
                        return CompareDate(date2) < 0;
                }

                int operator<=(const Date &date2) const    // Date1 <= Date2
                {
                        return CompareDate(date2) <= 0;
                }
};
...

// ----------- date08.h -----------
```

Again, note the presence of **const** and the passing by reference.
The main program follows:

```
// ----------- lab08.cpp -----------

#include <iostream.h>

#include "date08.h"

main()
{
        Date date1(90, 5, 6);
        Date date2(92, 1, 2);

        cout << "date1 == date2 " << (date1 == date2) << '\n';
        cout << "date1 != date2 " << (date1 != date2) << '\n';
        cout << "date1 < date2  " << (date1 < date2)  << '\n';
        cout << "date1 <= date2 " << (date1 <= date2) << '\n';
        cout << "date1 > date2  " << (date1 > date2)  << '\n';
        cout << "date1 >= date2 " << (date1 >= date2) << '\n';

        return 0;
}

// ----------- lab08.cpp -----------
```

The output produced is:

```
date1 == date2  0
date1 != date2  1
date1 <  date2  1
date1 <= date2  1
date1 >  date2  0
date1 >= date2  0
```

Exercise 9

The header includes a new **typedef** name to indicate the number of days between two dates, as well as the new operator functions, most of which are inlined:

```
// ----------- date09.h -----------

...
typedef int datediff_t;        // must be a signed integer type

class Date {
        ...
public:
        ...
// operators
        ...
        Date operator+(datediff_t incr) const;    // Date + integer

        friend Date operator+(datediff_t incr, const Date &date)
        {                                          // integer + Date
                return date + incr;
        }
```

We need a **friend** function to handle the construct *integer* + **Date**, because the left operand is not an object of class **Date**. However, because we want addition to be commutative, we can easily define this in terms of **Date** + *integer*.

```
        Date operator-(datediff_t decr) const;    // Date - integer

        datediff_t operator-(const Date &date2) const;  //Date1-Date2

        Date operator+=(datediff_t incr)           // Date += n
        {
                return *this = *this + incr;
        }
```

```
                Date operator-=(datediff_t decr)        // Date -= n
                {
                        return *this = *this - decr;
                }

                Date operator++()                       // ++Date
                {
                        return *this += 1;
                }

                Date operator++(int dummy)              // Date++
                {
                        Date TempDate = *this;

                        *this += 1;
                        return TempDate;
                }

                Date operator--()                       // --Date
                {
                        return *this -= 1;
                }

                Date operator--(int dummy)              // Date--
                {
                        Date TempDate = *this;

                        *this -= 1;
                        return TempDate;
                }
};
...

// ----------- date09.h -----------
```

The program follows:

```
// ----------- lab09.cpp -----------

#include <iostream.h>
#include <iomanip.h>

#include "date09.h"
```

```
main()
{
        Date date1(92, 2, 28);
        date1.print("date1                  ");
        Date date2;
        Date date3;

        date2 = date1 + 4;
        date2.print("date2 = date1 + 4    ");

        date2 = 400 + date1;
        date2.print("date2 = 400 + date1");

        date2 = date1 - 4;
        date2.print("date2 = date1 - 4    ");

        date2 = date1 - -4;
        date2.print("date2 = date1 - -4   ");

        date2 = date1 + -4;
        date2.print("date2 = date1 + -4   ");

        cout << '\n';
        date2 = date1++;
        date2.print("date2 = date1++      ");
        date1.print("date1                ");

        date2 = ++date1;
        date2.print("date2 = ++date1      ");
        date1.print("date1                ");

        date2 = date1--;
        date2.print("date2 = date1--      ");
        date1.print("date1                ");

        date2 = --date1;
        date2.print("date2 = --date1      ");
        date1.print("date1                ");

        cout << '\n';
        date2 += 5;
        date2.print("date2 += 5           ");

        date2 -= 5;
        date2.print("date2 -= 5           ");
```

```
                cout << '\n';
                date1 = Date(92,  3,  1);
                date2 = Date(91, 12,  1);
                date3 = Date(80,  5,  7);

                date1.print("date1                    ");
                date2.print("date2                    ");
                date3.print("date3                    ");

                cout << '\n';
                cout << "date1 - date2 " << (date1 - date2) << '\n';
                cout << "date2 - date1 " << (date2 - date1) << '\n';
                cout << "date1 - date3 " << (date1 - date3) << '\n';
                cout << "date3 - date1 " << (date3 - date1) << '\n';
                cout << "date2 - date3 " << (date2 - date3) << '\n';
                cout << "date3 - date2 " << (date3 - date2) << '\n';
                cout << "date2 - date2 " << (date2 - date2) << '\n';

                return 0;
        }

        Date Date::operator+(datediff_t incr) const        // Date + integer
        {
                if (incr < 0) {                            // watch for neg inc
                        return *this - -incr;
                }

                if (incr == 0) {
                        return *this;
                }

                Date TempDate = *this;
                day_t dd = GetDay();
                month_t mm = GetMonth();
                year_t yy = GetYear();
                int leapflag;

                for (datediff_t x = 1; x <= incr; ++x) {
                        leapflag = isleapyear(yy);

                        if (++dd <= GetDaysInMonth(leapflag, mm)) {//Month chg?
                                TempDate.SetDay(dd);               // no
                        }
```

```
                else {                                  // yes
                        TempDate.SetDay(dd = 1);
                        if (++mm <= 12) {               // Year chg?
                                TempDate.SetMonth(mm);  // no
                        }

                        else {                          // yes
                                TempDate.SetMonth(mm = 1);
                                TempDate.SetYear(++yy);
                        }
                }
        }

        return TempDate;
}
```

The method used to add an integer to a date is rather heavy-handed. To add n, we simply add 1 n times. You might be able to figure out a better approach, but by this time you should probably start thinking about whether storing a date as separate year, month, and day members is the best approach. If it were stored as a year and Julian day, certain operations would be simpler, and if it were stored as a "super" Julian day that included the year as well, things might be simplified even more.

The code continues:

```
Date Date::operator-(datediff_t decr) const    // Date - integer
{
        if (decr < 0) {                                 // watch for neg dec
                return *this + -decr;
        }


        if (decr == 0) {
                return *this;
        }


        Date TempDate = *this;
        day_t dd = GetDay();
        month_t mm = GetMonth();
        year_t yy = GetYear();
        int leapflag;
```

```
                for (datediff_t x = 1; x <= decr; ++x) {
                        leapflag = isleapyear(yy);

                        if (--dd >= 1) {                        // Month chg?
                                TempDate.SetDay(dd);            // no
                        }
                        else {                                  // yes
                                TempDate.SetDay(dd = GetDaysInMonth(leapflag,
                                        mm == 1 ? 12 : mm - 1));
                                if (--mm >= 1) {                // Year chg?
                                        TempDate.SetMonth(mm);  // no
                                }

                                else {                          // yes
                                        TempDate.SetMonth(mm = 12);
                                        TempDate.SetYear(--yy);
                                }
                        }
                }

                return TempDate;
        }
```

The same approach is taken here as was used in adding an integer to a date. To subtract n, we simply subtract 1 n times.

```
        datediff_t Date::operator-(const Date &date2) const // Date1 - Date2
        {
                Date TempDate1;
                Date TempDate2;
                int negflag;
                datediff_t daycount;

                if (*this < date2) {                    // need to swap over?
                        TempDate1 = date2;
                        TempDate2 = *this;
                        negflag = -1;
                }

                else if (*this == date2) {
                        return 0;
                }
```

```
            else {
                    TempDate1 = *this;
                    TempDate2 = date2;
                    negflag = 1;
            }

            day_t dd1 = TempDate1.GetDay();
            day_t dd2 = TempDate2.GetDay();
            month_t mm1 = TempDate1.GetMonth();
            month_t mm2 = TempDate2.GetMonth();
            year_t yy1 = TempDate1.GetYear();
            year_t yy2 = TempDate2.GetYear();

            julian_t jul1 = mdtojul(yy1, mm1, dd1);
            julian_t jul2 = mdtojul(yy2, mm2, dd2);

            if (yy1 == yy2) {
                    return negflag * (jul1 - jul2);
            }

            else {                      // yy1 must be > yy2 'cos of swap

                    daycount = (isleapyear(yy2) ? 366 : 365) - jul2 + jul1;
                    while (yy1 > ++yy2) {
                            daycount += (isleapyear(yy2) ? 366 : 365);
                    }
                    return negflag * daycount;
            }
}

// ---------- lab09.cpp ----------
```

The output produced is:

```
Date date1              is 28-Feb-1992
Date date2 = date1 + 4    is 03-Mar-1992
Date date2 = 400 + date1  is 03-Apr-1993
Date date2 = date1 - 4    is 24-Feb-1992
Date date2 = date1 - -4   is 03-Mar-1992
Date date2 = date1 + -4   is 24-Feb-1992

Date date2 = date1++      is 28-Feb-1992
Date date1                is 29-Feb-1992
Date date2 = ++date1      is 01-Mar-1992
Date date1                is 01-Mar-1992
Date date2 = date1--      is 01-Mar-1992
```

```
Date date1              is 29-Feb-1992
Date date2 = --date1    is 28-Feb-1992
Date date1              is 28-Feb-1992

Date date2 += 5         is 04-Mar-1992
Date date2 -= 5         is 28-Feb-1992

Date date1              is 01-Mar-1992
Date date2              is 01-Dec-1991
Date date3              is 07-May-1980

date1 - date2 91
date2 - date1 -91
date1 - date3 4316
date3 - date1 -4316
date2 - date3 4225
date3 - date2 -4225
date2 - date2 0
```

Exercise 10

The header now includes the I/O operator functions:

```
// ----------- date10.h -----------

...
class Date {
        ...
public:
        ...
// operators
        ...
        friend istream &operator>>(istream &istr, Date &date);

        friend ostream &operator<<(ostream &ostr, const Date &date);
};
...

// ----------- date10.h -----------
```

The program follows:

```
// ----------- lab10.cpp -----------

#include <iostream.h>
#include <iomanip.h>

#include "date10.h"

main()
{
        Date date1;

        cin >> date1;
        cout << "date1 = |" << date1 << "|\n";

        return 0;
}

// >> can handle a date with format mm/dd/[yy]yy only, where leading
// zeros are ignored.

istream &operator>>(istream &istr, Date &date)
{
        int yy = YEAR_DEFAULT;
        int mm = MONTH_DEFAULT;
        int dd = DAY_DEFAULT;
        char c;

        cin >> setbase(10) >> mm >> c >> dd >> c >> yy;

        date.SetYear((yy >= 0 && yy < 100) ? yy + 1900 : yy);
        date.SetMonth(mm);
        date.SetDay(dd);

        return istr;
}
```

As mentioned above with respect to in-memory string decoding, we need temporaries here; we cannot simply read into the date members directly. Also, we must be careful not to use the types **day_t** and **month_t** for **dd** and **mm**, since these types might be character types resulting in character I/O rather than integer I/O, as mentioned earlier.

The **setbase** manipulator is necessary to handle numbers larger than 7 that have leading zeros. By default, the standard library input routines treat integers the same as integer constants: A leading 0 means octal and a leading 0x or 0X means hex. By explicitly telling **setbase** to use base 10 (decimal) mode, we cause leading zeros to be ignored. Without the manipulator, a month of 08 would be taken as month 0, and the 8 would be taken as the separator character:

Exercise 10

```
ostream &operator<<(ostream &ostr, const Date &date)
{
        ostr << setw(2) << setfill('0')
            << (display_t)date.GetDay() << "-"
            << Date::GetMonthNamesAbbrev(date.GetMonth())
            << "-" << date.GetYear();

        return ostr;
}

// ----------- lab10.cpp -----------
```

Some sample inputs and outputs follow:

09/08/1923
date1 = |08-Sep-1923|

3/2/91
date1 = |02-Mar-1991|

Recommended Reading

The following books and publications provide useful information on object-oriented design and programming in general, C++ in particular, and the terminology invented and/or used by the C and C++ standards committees.

Books

- Booch, Grady. *Object-Oriented Design with Applications*. Redwood City, CA: Benjamin Cummings, 1991.

- Cargill, Tom. *C++ Programming Style*. Reading, MA: Addison-Wesley, 1992.

- Coplien, James O. *Advanced C++ Programming Styles and Idioms*. Reading, MA: Addison-Wesley, 1992.

- Dewhurst, Stephen C., and Kathryn T. Stark. *Programming in C++*. Englewood Cliffs, NJ: Prentice Hall, 1989.

- Ellis, Margaret A., and Bjarne Stroustrup. *The Annotated C++ Reference Manual*. Reading, MA: Addison-Wesley, 1991.

- Gorlen, Keith E., Sanford M. Orlow, and Perry S. Plexico. *Data Abstraction and Object-Oriented Programming in C++*. Somerset, NJ: John Wiley and Sons, 1990.

    This book describes an extensive public-domain class library and indicates where a copy can be obtained.

- Jaeschke, Rex. *The Dictionary of Standard C*. Horsham, PA: CBM Books (formerly Professional Press Books), 1992.

- Lipman, Stanley B. *C++ Primer*, 2nd ed. Reading, MA: Addison-Wesley, 1991.

- Meyers, Scott. *Effective C++: 50 Specific Ways to Improve Your Programs and Designs*. Reading, MA: Addison-Wesley, 1992.

- Shlaer, Sally, and Stephen J. Mellor. *Object Lifecycles: Modeling the World in States*. Englewood Cliffs, NJ: Prentice Hall, 1992.

- Shlaer, Sally, and Stephen J. Mellor. *Object-Oriented Systems Analysis: Modeling the World in Data*. Englewood Cliffs, NJ: Prentice Hall, 1988.

- Stroustrup, Bjarne. *The C++ Programming Language*, 2nd ed. Reading, MA: Addison-Wesley, 1991.

- Taylor, David A. *Object-Oriented Technology*. Reading, MA: Addison-Wesley, 1990.

Publications

- *C++ Journal*. Port Washington, NY: The C++ Journal Inc.

- (Draft) *C++ Language Standard*, Standards Committees X3J16 and WG21. X3 Secretariat, 1250 Eye Street, NW, Ste. 200, Washington, DC 20005.

- *C++ Report*. New York, NY: SIGS Publications.

- *C Users Journal*. Lawrence, KS: R&D Publications.

- *Dr. Dobbs Journal*. San Mateo, CA: M&T Publishing.

Index

Symbols
++, postfix versus prefix, 179
, (comma), 144
--, postfix versus prefix, 179
->, 144
->*, 97
.*, 97, 144
. (dot), 144
::, *See* scope resolution operator
<<, 4
    overloading of, 161
=, *See* assignment
>>, 4
    embedded white space and, 4
    leading white space and, 4
    overloading of, 161
?:, 144
&
    operator, 144
    reference punctuator, 35
~ (tilde), *See* destructor

A
abnormal program termination, **new** and, 134
abort, destructor and, 133
access specifier, 77
    nested classes and, 93
alias, *See* reference
Annotated C++ Reference Manual, xi
anonymous union, 11
    linkage, 12
    member function and, 91
    restrictions on, 91
app, 69
argument matching, 17
    rules for, 17
argument passing
    by address, 33
    by reference, 33, 34
    by value, 33
argument type, restriction on, 185
argument value, default, 20
ARM, *See Annotated C++ Reference Manual*
array
    bounds checking, 156
    initializer for class, 123
asm, 181
assignment, 144
ate, 69
auto, 181

B
bad, 67
beg, 70
binary, 69
bit-field, 91
    reference and, 44
break, 181
    destructor and, 133

C
C++
    compatibility with C, 185
    future of, xi
    mixing with other languages, 7
    release history, xi
    successor to C, xi
case, 181
cast
    function notation form, 9

functional notation form
    overloading, 170
    reference type and, 45
    restriction on, 185
catch, 176, 181
cerr, 4
    buffering and, 4
char, 181
character constant, type of, 17, 185
cin, 4, 161
    scanf versus, 4
class, 49, 77
    derived, 175
    enclosing, *See* enclosing class
    local
        member function restrictions, 92
        restrictions on, 92
    member of reference type, 124
    name, scope of local, 92
    nested, *See* nested class
    structure, comparison with, 91
    union, comparison with, 91
class, 77, 181
class library, 49
class member
    const, 124
    function, *See* member function
    private, 77
        accessing, 79
    public, 77
    reference type, of, 124
    relaxing access restrictions, *See* friend function
    restricting access to, 78
    static data, 84
        storage allocation for, 85
clear, 67
clog, 4
close, 68
comments, 3
const, 181
    data member, 124
    when it means constant, 11, 186
const object

initializer, 11
linkage, 11
const-qualified function, 87
    restriction on calls from, 89
    restriction on calls to, 88
    static data members and, 89
constructor, 51, 119
    call order
        across modules, 132
        array, 131
        automatic data, 129
        static data, 129
    const, 123
    conversion, *See* conversion constructor
    copy, *See* copy constructor
    default, *See* default constructor
    file I/O, standard, 69
    having one argument, 121
    initializing const member, 125
    istrstream, 71
    name of, 119
    nested class and, 126
    new and, 135
    ostrstream, 71
    restrictions on, 123
    return type of, 120
    static, 123
    taking the address of, 123
    union and, 123
    utility of, 123
    volatile, 123
    when called, 123
continue, 181
    destructor and, 133
conversion constructor, 121
conversion function, 170
copy constructor, 168
copying objects, 165
cout, 4, 161
    comparison with printf, 4
__cplusplus, 7
cur, 70

Index

D
`dec`, 60, 64
`default`, 181
default argument, 20
    information accumulation, 21
    nonconstant value, 110
        binding of, 110
    overloading and, 21
    pointer to function and, 21
default constructor, 52, 120
    array initialization and, 124
    `new`, 136
`delete`, 27, 181
    overloading of, 159
    scope resolution operator and, 140
    user-defined version of, 140
derived class, 175
destructor, 53, 119
    `abort` and, 133
    `break` and, 133
    call order
        across modules, 132
        array, 131
        automatic data, 129
        static data, 129
    `const`, 123
    `continue` and, 133
    `delete` and, 135
    `exit` and, 133
    `goto` and, 133
    `longjmp` and, 133
    name of, 122
    nested class and, 126
    overloading and, 122
    restrictions on, 123
    return type of, 122
    `static`, 123
    `switch` and, 133
    taking the address of, 123
    union and, 123
    utility of, 123
    `volatile`, 123
    when called, 123
`do`, 181
`double`, 181
dynamic memory
    allocation of, 27
    mixing C and C++, 30

E
`else`, 181
encapsulation, 77
enclosing class, 92
`end`, 70
`endl`, 61
`ends`, 61
`enum`, 181
enumerated type
    class-specific, 90
    compatibility with integer types, 12, 13, 185
    performing I/O on, 13
enumeration constant, type of, 185
`eof`, 67
error detection, member function, 67
error handler for `new`, 30
exception handling, ix, 31, 176
`exit`, destructor and, 133
`extern`, 181
    reference to, 45
`extern "C"`, 7
`extern "C++"`, 7
external names, disambiguating duplicate, *See* name mangling
extraction, 4

F
`fail`, 67
`fgetpos`, 69
`fgets`, 65
`__FILE__`, inline function and, 23
file I/O, *See* I/O, file
file open mode bits, 69
`fill`, 67
`fixed`, 64
`flags`, 63
`float`, 181
`flush`, 61

for, 181
    first expression in, 8
format state, 63
    flags, 63
fread, 66
friend, 95, 181
friend class, 96
friend function, 95, 146, 150, 162
    inlining and, 117
fseek, 69
fsetpos, 69
fstream, 67
    default open mode, 69
fstream.h, 67
ftell, 69
function
    const-qualified, *See* const-qualified function
    conversion, 170
    friend, *See* friend function
    inline, 22
    member, *See* member function
    non-C++ linkage, overloading and, 15
    non-void, return and, 5
    old-style declaration, 186
    old-style definition, 186
    returning a reference, 38
    volatile-qualified, *See* volatile-qualified function
function argument, hidden, *See* this
function linkage
    external, 79
    internal, 79
function notation cast, 9
function signature, *See* signature
fwrite, 66

G
gcount, 66
get, 65, 66
getchar, 65
getline, 65
global data, class-specific, 84
good, 67

goto, 181
    destructor and, 133

H
header
    I/O, 3
    standard, *See* fstream.h, iomanip.h, iostream.h, new.h, strstream.h
hex, 60, 64

I
identifier, length of significance, 3, 185
if, 181
ifstream, 67
ignore, 66
in, 69
    input streams and, 69
inheritance, ix, 175
    multiple, 176
    single, 176
initialization
    bypass, attempts to, 134
    new and, 137
initializer
    array and new, 138
    array of class, 123
    char array using string, 186
    class object, *See* constructor
    const member, 125
    const object, 11
    default, array of class, 124
inline, 22, 181
inline function, 22
    __FILE__ and, 23
    __LINE__ and, 24
    linkage of, 23, 112
    macro versus, 24
    member, 112
    taking the address of, 22
inlining
    compiler options and, 25
    debugging and, 25
    disabling and enabling, 24
    friend function and, 117

insertion, 4
instance, 79
instantiation, 79
`int`, 181
`internal`, 64
I/O
    buffering and, 61
    `char *`, 60
    `char *` versus `void *`, 60
    controlling format, *See* manipulator
    file, 67
        disk, 67
    header, standard, 3
    member function, standard, 66
    output format
        default, 59
        overriding default, 60
    pointer to member and, 101
    random positioning, 69
    standard class, `ios`, 69, 70
    standard, `ios`, 64
    stream
        standard file, 67
    `void *` versus `char *`, 60
iomanip.h, 61, 73
IOMANIPdeclare, 74
`ios`, 64, 69, 70
iostream.h, 3, 59, 161
`istream`, 161
`istrstream`, 71

J
jumping into a block, 134, 185

K
keywords
    archaic, *See* `overload`
    C++-specific, 181, 185
    table of, 181

L
`left`, 64
__LINE__, inline function and, 24
linkage
    `const` object, 11

    non-C++, 7
local class, 92
    member function in, 117
`long`, 181
`longjmp`, destructor and, 133
lvalue
    cast operator returning, 45
    function call operator returning, 39

M
macro
    inline function versus, 24
    predefined, *See* __cplusplus
`main`
    overloading and, 15
    restrictions on, 185
mangling, *See* name mangling
manipulator, 60
    lifetime of effect, 61
    standard
        with no arguments, 61
        with one argument, 61
    user-defined
        multiple arguments, 74
        no arguments, 72
        one argument, 73
member, *See* class member
member function, 55
    anonymous union and, 91
    constructor, *See* constructor
    definition of, 80
    destructor, *See* destructor
    error detection, 67
    how to call, 80
    inline, 92, 112
        forward reference from, 117
    I/O, standard, 66
    local class, 117
    name, duplicates across classes, 81
    private, 82
    stream, standard, 64
member name, conflict with local name, 104

N

name mangling, 7
    disabling, 7
    overloaded functions and, 108
    pointer to function and, 7
nested class, 92
    constructors and, 126
    destructors and, 126
    name
      scope of, 92
      `typedef` and, 94
`new`, 27, 181
    abnormal program termination and, 134
    array initializer and, 138
    constructor and, 135
    default constructor and, 136
    destructor and, 135
    error handler for, 30
    initialization and, 137
    overloading of, 159
    scope resolution operator and, 140
    user-defined version of, 140
    zero byte allocation and, 30
`new.h`, 31
`nocreate`, 69
`noreplace`, 69

O

`oct`, 60, 64
`ofstream`, 67
old-style function declaration, 186
old-style function definition, 186
`OMANIP`, 73
`open`, 68
operator
    address-of, 144
    assignment, 144
    built-in, properties of, 144
    comma, 144
    `delete`, 27
    function call, lvalue and, 39
    member selection, 144
    `new`, 27
    not overloadable, 144
    overloaded
      associativity of, 144
      operand count, 144
      precedence of, 144
      predefined, 144
      type of result, 144
    overloading, 143
      !=, 145
      + (binary), 147
      ++ (postfix), 154
      ++ (prefix), 153
      +=, 151
      - (unary), 152
      -- (postfix), 154
      -- (prefix), 153
      <<, 161
      =, 169
      ==, 145
      >>, 161
      [ ], 155
      ( ), 157
      advice on, 171
      assignment, 165
      cast, 170
      commutativity and, 150
      `delete`, 159
      `new`, 159
      unary, 152
    pointer to member, *See* ->* and .*
    precedence, 179
    scope resolution, *See* scope resolution operator
`operator`, 181
operator overloading, *See* operator, overloading, 4
`ostream`, 161
`ostrstream`, 71
`out`, 69
    output streams and, 69
output
    buffered, *See* `clog`
    unbuffered, *See* `cerr`
`overload`, 184
overloaded functions

name mangling and, 108
reference argument and, 37
type qualifiers and, 108
overloading, 15
    default argument and, 21
    function, 15
        member, 106
    `main` and, 15
    non-C++ linkage function and, 15
    operator, *See* operator, overloading, 4

P
`peek`, 66
pointer
    reference to, 42, 45
    reference versus, 45
pointer to member, 96
    compatibility with other pointers, 96
    conversion of, 96
    I/O and, 101
    operators, *See* ->* and .*
pointer to overloaded function, 18
polymorphism, ix, 176
precedence of operators, 179
`precision`, 67
`private`, 79, 181
`protected`, 176, 181
`public`, 77, 181
`put`, 65
`putback`, 66
`putchar`, 65

R
R1.0, xi
R2.0, xi
R2.1, xi
    compatibility with old releases, 183
R3.0, xi
`rdstate`, 67
`read`, 66
reference, 33
    argument passing by, 34
    array element and, 43
    array of, 45
    to bit-field, 44
    cast to, 45
    class member having type, 124
    to `extern`, 45
    outside argument list, 39
    to pointer, 42
    pointer to, 45
    pointer versus, 45
    to reference, 42
    restrictions on, 45
    return from a function, 38
    structure or union member and, 43
    `typedef` in, 44
    to variable, 39
    to `void`, 45
reference argument
    constant as, 37
    overloaded functions and, 37
    type compatibility, 37
reference punctuator `&`, 35
`register`, 181
`resetiosflags`, 61
`return`, 181
    non-void function and, 5
return type, restriction on, 185
`right`, 64

S
`scanf`
    `cin` versus, 4
`scientific`, 64
scope resolution operator, 82, 86, 91, 144
    `delete` and, 140
    `new` and, 140
SEEK_CUR, 70
SEEK_END, 70
`seekg`, 70
`seekp`, 70
SEEK_SET, 70
`set_new_handler`, 31
`setbase`, 61
`setf`, 64
`setfill`, 61, 67
`setiosflags`, 61

setprecision, 61, 67
setw, 60, 67
short, 181
showbase, 64
showpoint, 64
showpos, 64
signature, 7
signed, 181
sizeof, 181
    restriction on, 185
skipws, 64
sprintf, 70
sscanf, 70
Standard C++, base documents, xi
static, 181
static data member
    accessing public using ::, 86
    definition of, 85
    storage allocation for, 85, 86
static function member, 86
stderr, 4
stdin, 4
stdio, 64
stdout, 4
stream, 3
stream member function, standard, 64
string decoding, 70
string encoding, 70
Stroustrup, Bjarne, xi
strstream.h, 70
struct, 77, 181
structure tag, scope of nested, 186
structure, compared with class, 91
switch, 181
    destructor and, 133

T
tellg, 70
tellp, 70
template, 175, 181
templates, ix, xi, 175
temporary object
    creation by constructor, 134
    evaluation order, 135
    lifetime of, 135
this, 81, 104, 181
    explicit use of, 104, 105
    scope of, 104
    type of, 106
throw, 176, 181
trunc, 69
try, 176, 181
typedef, 181
    class-specific, 90
    nested class name and, 94
    of a reference, 44
type-safe linkage, 7

U
union
    anonymous, *See* anonymous union
    class, comparison with, 91
    constructor and, 123
    destructor and, 123
    restrictions on, 91
union, 181
union tag, scope of nested, 186
unitbuf, 64
unnamed object, *See* temporary object
unsetf, 64
unsigned, 181
uppercase, 64

V
virtual, 176, 181
virtual function, 176
void, 181
void *, 96
volatile, 181
volatile-qualified function, 87
    restriction on calls from, 89
    restriction on calls to, 88

W
while, 181
width, 67
write, 66
ws, 61

Complete your C Library with the Jaeschke Collection

Rex Jaeschke, the Master of C, explains it all for you.

Now you can know as much about C and C++ as Rex Jaeschke, the internationally known C author and seminar leader. These user-friendly books give you all the C information you need at your fingertips. The Jaeschke Collection is renowned by computing professionals around the world — and now you can own the complete set.

C++: An Introduction for Experienced C Programmers

Softcover, 240 pages
Order extra copies and save (see order form).

Includes: ■ Classes ■ Functions ■ Keywords ■ Constructors and Destructors ■ Elementary I/O ■ Dynamic Memory Allocation ■ References ■ Operator Overloading ■ Problems and Worked Solutions ■ Recommended Reading

Mastering Standard C: A Self-Paced Training Course in Modern C

Softcover, 366 pages
Self-paced, self teaching tutorial.

Includes: ■ Looping & Testing ■ Arrays ■ Functions ■ Identifier Scope and Life ■ The C Preprocessor ■ Pointers ■ Structures, Bit-Fields and Unions ■ C's Typing Mechanism ■ Standard Run-time Library ■ Appendices

Portability And The C Language

Softcover, 382 pages
For moving C around.

Includes: ■ Lexical Elements ■ Conversions ■ Expressions ■ Declarations ■ Statements ■ The C Preprocessor ■ The C Run-time Library ■ Keywords & Reserved Identifiers ■ Portability Software Suite

The Dictionary of Standard C

Softcover, 165 pages
A to Z definitions of Standard C language terminology.

Includes: ■ Concise Definitions of Standard C Terms ■ Library Functions ■ Cross-Referenced Entries ■ ANSI C Standard Compliant ■ Mini-Tutorials

CBM BOOKS

Rex Jaeschke is a member of ANSI C++ Standards Committee X3J16 and is the U.S. Head-of-Delegation to the ISO C committee WG14. He is also covener and chair of the Numerical C Extensions Group (X3J11.1), a committee developing extensions to C for use by numerical programmers. Jaeschke is also C and C++ editor for *DEC Professional* magazine.

To order, use the form on the other side.

Or use these fast, easy order options:

■ By phone (215) 957-4265
■ By FAX (215) 957-1050
■ Through CompuServe #76702,1565

The Jaeschke Collection *Order Form*

Simply complete and return — or pass it on to a colleague!

Title	Qty	Subtotal
C++: An Introduction for Experienced C Programmers		
1-5 copies: $30 each!		
6-15 copies: $25.50 each! Save 15%!		
16-49 copies: $21 each! Save 30%!		
50+ copies: $18 each! Save 40%!		
Mastering Standard C: A Self-Paced Training Course in Modern C $40		
Portability And The C Language $19		
The Dictionary of Standard C $17		
PA residents add 6% sales tax.		
UPS shipping: $4 for the first book, $1 for each additional book. Outside the U.S., please call (215) 957-4265 for shipping information.		
TOTAL ORDER		

Special Offer: Order more copies of C++ and save!

☐ Check enclosed for $_____.

Charge to: ☐ MasterCard   ☐ VISA   ☐ American Express

Account #: _____ Exp. Date _____

Signature _____ Date _____

Name _____

Title _____

Company _____

Address (street address required) _____

City _____ State _____ Zip _____

Country _____

Telephone (____) _____ FAX (____) _____

☐ Please send me a free CBM Books catalog.

Mail to: CBM Books, P.O. Box 446, Horsham, PA 19044

Order by phone: (215) 957-4265
or
Order by fax: (215) 957-1050

CBM BOOKS